Strategic Culture
and Italy's Military Behavior

Strategic Culture and Italy's Military Behavior

Between Pacifism and Realpolitik

Paolo Rosa

LEXINGTON BOOKS
Lanham • Boulder • New York • London

Published by Lexington Books
An imprint of The Rowman & Littlefield Publishing Group, Inc.
4501 Forbes Boulevard, Suite 200, Lanham, Maryland 20706
www.rowman.com

Unit A, Whitacre Mews, 26-34 Stannary Street, London SE11 4AB

Copyright © 2016 by Lexington Books

All rights reserved. No part of this book may be reproduced in any form or by any electronic or mechanical means, including information storage and retrieval systems, without written permission from the publisher, except by a reviewer who may quote passages in a review.

British Library Cataloguing in Publication Information Available

Library of Congress Cataloging-in-Publication Data

Originally published in Italian as Tra pacifismo e realpolitik: Cultura strategica e politica estera in Italia in 2012 by Rubbettino.
First published in English by Lexington Books in 2016.
English translation copyright © 2016 by Lexington Books.

Names: Rosa, Paolo, 1963- author.
Title: Strategic culture and Italy's military behavior : between pacifism and realpolitik / Paolo Rosa.
Description: Lanham, MD : Lexington Books, [2016] | Includes bibliographical references and index.
Identifiers: LCCN 2016001271 (print) | LCCN 2016002335 (ebook) | ISBN 9781498522816 (cloth : alk. paper) | ISBN 9781498522823 (Electronic)
Subjects: LCSH: Italy--Foreign relations. | Strategic culture--Italy. | Italy--Military policy.
Classification: LCC DG583.5 .R67 2016 (print) | LCC DG583.5 (ebook) | DDC 327.45--dc23 LC record available at http://lccn.loc.gov/2016001271

∞™ The paper used in this publication meets the minimum requirements of American National Standard for Information Sciences Permanence of Paper for Printed Library Materials, ANSI/NISO Z39.48-1992.

Printed in the United States of America

To Mari and Franz

Contents

Acknowledgments ix

1 Introduction: Italy's Foreign Policy, Some Alternative Explanations 1

I: The Study of Strategic Culture in International Relations 15

2 The Sociological Turn in International Relations 17
3 The Study of Strategic Cultures 31

II: Italy's Strategic Culture and Foreign Policy 59

4 Italy's Strategic Culture 61
5 Italy's Strategic Culture and International Behavior 95
6 Conclusions 129

Bibliography 135
Index 143
About the Author 147

Acknowledgments

This publication was supported by the *Programma di Interesse Nazionale* (PRIN) of the Italian Ministry of Education (Title: *La politica estera italiana di fronte alle nuove minacce del sistema internazionale: attori, istituzioni e politiche*), Grant Agreement n. 201032T8ZE_004.

I thank SAGE Publications for the permission to reproduce parts of my article: "The Accommodationist State: Strategic Culture and Italy's Military Behavior," *International Relations* 28(1), 2014.

ONE

Introduction

Italy's Foreign Policy, Some Alternative Explanations

Italy, although it considers itself a medium-sized power, like France, the United Kingdom, and Germany, has been incapable of playing a political role comparable to theirs on the international stage, pursuing a low-profile foreign policy throughout the Cold War period. This cannot be attributed entirely to material constraints,[1] given that the low profile was consistently maintained both in times of economical crisis and of economical growth. Rather, it is the result of the country's strategic culture, which is a mix of *realpolitik* and pacifist elements. Notwithstanding changes in military technology, in the domestic political system and in the international structure, Italy's attitude towards the use of force has remained substantially the same: military power is viewed as a tool to be used with great circumspection in the pursuit of national interest, for exclusively defensive purposes and within a multilateral framework. Military spending has remained low, both in absolute terms and in comparison with the other medium-sized European powers; interventions abroad are still hotly debated politically and looked upon with suspicion. The aim of this book is to provide an in-depth analysis of how strategic culture has affected these behaviors.

EXPLANATIONS OF ITALY'S FOREIGN POLICY

Foreign policy scholars distinguish between the external and internal factors affecting the international behavior of a country (Beasley et al. 2002; Evangelista 1997). Among the external factors, the neorealist and neoliberal theories include international anarchy and the distribution of power, economic interdependence and the distribution of wealth, international cooperation and the multilateral institutions. The interpretations based on internal factors, as in the case of the liberal theories,[2] take into account such variables as the competition between political actors, the characteristics of the leaders, the decision-making processes, and the nature of the regimes. This distinction between external and internal interpretations may be useful in contextualizing the interpretation of the Italian foreign policy.[3]

One of the first scholars who tackled the issue of Italy's foreign policy in terms of external influences was Gianfranco Pasquino, in an article published in 1974 and titled *Pesi Internazionali e Contrappesi Nazionali*. Based on an analysis of the bipolar system of the postwar period, Pasquino claimed that Italy's foreign policy was strongly influenced by the constraints imposed by the Cold War. Confrontation between the United States and Soviet Union (USSR), and the inclusion of Italy in the U.S. sphere of influence, resulted in the country's decision-making agenda being dictated by the global dynamics. Italy was obliged to play a marginal role on the international scene and to outsource its security to NATO (the Atlantic Alliance). Italy's role, within NATO, was that of a loyal—albeit passive—partner: Italian governments would rarely dissent from the decisions taken by the United States. Italy's subordinate position within the Western system prevented its European policy from becoming too independent vis-à-vis the Atlantic dimension. Italy was rather suspicious of the French Gaullist positions. This state of affairs, however, did not prevent Rome from specializing in several fields in which it could apply a foreign policy more independent with respect to its American ally, such as in the Mediterranean and in the Middle East.

The limitations imposed by the bipolar system obliged the political parties to modify their behavior and to redefine their policies, in order to make them more compatible externally. The Italian Socialist Party (PSI), for example, was compelled to abandon its neutralism in exchange for entering the government and becoming a reliable partner to the Christian Democrat party (DC). During the 1970s, the Communist Party (PCI), chaired by Enrico Berlinguer, changed its traditional anti-American stance in favor of support to NATO and the European Community.[4]

Ennio Di Nolfo highlights the influence of the international system on Italian politics, identifying the restrictions imposed on the freedom of action of the political leaders by Italy's inclusion in the Western subsystem. While primarily focusing on the impact of international politics on the domestic political system, his analysis is nevertheless interesting to understand the country's foreign policy.

Di Nolfo observes how the process of integration within the Western bloc was less rigid than in the Soviet-controlled bloc, thus enabling policy-makers to "choose" the method for adapting to the major ally's requests. He proposes a periodization of the domestic and international events, distinguishing between periods in which the external influence was highly compelling and periods in which the governments enjoyed more freedom of action (Di Nolfo 1979: 87–88).

- The 1942–1943 period was marked by the crisis of the Fascist regime. During this period the political elites became aware of the need to reestablish relations with the Western powers to save the country.
- The 1943–1944 period witnessed the loss of interest by the emerging leadership in the constraints imposed by the nascent international system, almost unaware of the fact that the world was on the eve of being partitioned into spheres of influence.
- The 1944–1946 period was marked by the collaboration between the *Resistance* movement and the allied forces and in the replacement of the myth of national independence with that of external subordination.
- The 1947–1953 period was characterized by the defeat of the Communist and Socialist Parties and by Italy becoming a member of NATO. In this phase the two blocs hardened their stance, with reduced leeway for the national governments.
- In the 1953–1958 period the hegemony of the DC started to falter. The experimentation of new government coalitions brought to light the limitations posed by the international balances on domestic decisions.
- The 1958–1963 period paved the way for the center-left government project and, internationally, the thawing of East-West relations.
- The 1963–1968 period witnessed the formation of center-left governments and the redefinition, by the Socialist Party, of a new international policy line, which became more pro-Atlantic.
- The post-1968 period was marked by the beginning of a political crisis in Italy and by profound changes in international politics (détente, strategic armaments limitation treaties, rapprochement in U.S.–China relations).

In all these stages, Di Nolfo reconstructs the processes whereby Italian policy making adapted to the international dynamics, revealing how politicians managed to creatively interpret these constraints, albeit never to the point of questioning the strategic interests of the United States. At two key turning points—in the 1960s, with the formation of the center-left governments, and in the 1970s, with the prospect of the Communists entering the government—external pressure became very strong and the leeway for independent decision making was significantly reduced.

While recognizing that this external influence did not affect Italy alone, but all the former European powers to a greater or lesser degree, Di Nolfo does highlight certain peculiarities in the case of Italy (Di Nolfo 1977: 105):

The Italian case is similar to countless other examples of the so-called small and medium-sized powers. However, it is also unique, if one considers that Italy alone, among the former European powers, remains a State with such a fragile political system, to the point that links with the international system were more frequently established, and the capacity to use these links for the purpose of solving Italy's domestic problems often had to give way to the interests of others actors that have different priorities prevailing over that of the Italian partner. In other words, the specific problems of Italy had to be sacrificed to external needs.

The broadest analysis of Italy's foreign policy, focusing on the external variables, has been made by Carlo Maria Santoro (1991). Santoro identifies several deeply-rooted forces (permanent factors) that affect Italian foreign policy. These are related to the international environment, Italy's geographical position and historical traditions. The inputs from the domestic environment, to which he dedicates much less space, play a secondary role. The analysis of domestic dynamics is limited to a description of the *foreign policy community*, consisting of actors who are more or less distant from the decision-making center.

He splits up the international environment into a global system and a regional subsystem. The global system influences Italy's foreign policy through a number of processes that are related to power diffusion phenomena: that is, the weakening of the military blocs and the emergence of a greater freedom of action for the medium/small powers.

Alongside the global processes, Santoro singles out a series of decisive factors stemming from the regional subsystem: thanks to its role as a bridge between Europe, Africa, and the Near East, Italy can play a more incisive role at this level. In the Mediterranean Basin, Santoro identifies four areas of interest for Italy at the intersection between the North/South and East/West axes. By intervening along these axes, Italy can express different degrees of freedom and varied behavior. The four subsystems are: (1) the Balkans, comprising the former Warsaw Pact member countries; (2) North Africa, comprising Libya and the Maghreb countries; (3) the Middle East, comprising Israel and the Persian Gulf countries; and (4) the Euro-Atlantic system, comprising the NATO and the EU (European Union).

The second "permanent factor" in Italy's foreign policy is geography. The geographical factor is the one that "more than any other defines the field, as well as the range of opportunities, available to a country like Italy, and which is subject to changes less than any other" (Ibid.: 47).[5] The country's geographical peculiarity—an appendage of Europe jutting into the Mediterranean—fuels a twofold continental and maritime vocation, which is not always accomplished in a consistent manner.[6] This situation drives Italy to intervene in different areas simultaneously, without having the resources for such an all-round diplomacy, and pursuing interests that are sometimes disconnected or even contradictory.

After World War II, Italy's foreign policy unfolded at three different concentric levels (Garruccio 1982): the Atlantic, by joining NATO and adopting a passive attitude towards the United States; Europe, by joining the European Community from the beginning and adopting a strongly integrationist approach, although its rhetoric surpassed the achievement of any concrete results, given Italy's economic and institutional backwardness; and lastly, the Mediterranean, viewed as an area of immense strategic importance due to the country's dependency on energy imports from the Middle East and North Africa. During the Cold War, Italy's image as a far corner of Europe prevailed over that of a peninsula in the middle of the Mediterranean.

Alongside the structure of the international system and the geographical position, Santoro identifies five historical traditions affecting Italy's foreign policy. First, Italy's position in the international hierarchy. Since the country's unification, Italy appeared an anomaly, being included among the European great powers as an act of international "courtesy" rather than because of its actual political weight. Even in the illustrations of the time, Italy is portrayed as a gracious lady kept to the sidelines by the other superpowers, depicted as very martial-looking men.[7] Federico Chabod (1965), in his classic analysis of the foundations of Italy's foreign policy, highlights how the country soon found itself in a predicament, aspiring to be recognized as a superpower, on a par with France, the United Kingdom, Germany, Austria-Hungary, and Russia, while at the same time failing to allocate the necessary financial and military resources that would have enabled it to accomplish this aspiration.[8] The same problem resurfaced after World War II, when Italy's role oscillated between being the largest of the small powers and the smallest of the large.

The second historical tradition is related to the concept of security. For Santoro, Italy has always struggled between a spasmodic search for alliances to solve its security problems (the Triple Alliance in the Liberal period and NATO and the EU in the Republican period), and the specular fear of being dragged into wars that might conflict with its national interest.

The third historical tradition is the multiplicity of the foreign policy objectives. Italian policymakers, for various reasons, including the geographical position mentioned earlier, have proved unable to define a clear national interest and a geographical area of major strategic interest for the country. This has produced improvised policies, an excessive diversification of initiatives, and a waste of resources scattered aimlessly.

The fourth historical factor concerns the fact that the international objectives are often—and willingly—subordinated to domestic priorities.

Finally, the last historical tradition is related to the conduct of diplomacy, which is characterized by reactivity—it is stimulated by initiatives put into place by others—and a great deal of opportunism, typical of a small rather than a great/middle power.

Since the end of the Cold War, several studies have been produced on Italy's foreign policy based on the external factors (Pirani 2004: 4–7). According to these studies, the end of the bipolar confrontation has led to the emergence of new opportunities for medium-sized powers, opening up room for maneuvers that were unthinkable at the time of the opposition between blocs. The weakening of the Atlantic Alliance encouraged Italy, which had always played a passive role under the American strategic umbrella, to become more active in furthering its interests. Thus, from the early 1990s, Italy started to play a more active international role, taking part in important conflicts, such as the First Gulf War, the campaign in Kosovo, and the armed interventions in Iraq and Afghanistan. The redefinition of the international order fostered a transition from a *security taker* to a *security provider* role, boosting Italy's participation in peacekeeping/peace-building missions.[9] This activism offered the framework for reforming the Italian Armed Forces, consisting in the abolition of the previous conscription-based system and the introduction of a professional force.

The problem with the interpretation based on external factors is that the material international structures have an ambiguous effect on a country's foreign policy. They can encourage one type of behavior or its opposite. To understand the direction taken, we need to observe the ideational factors. "Distribution of material capabilities and their systematic effects are indeterminate; their effects are determined by intersubjective interpretation" (Johnston 1998a: 69), that is, the "shared expectations about appropriate behavior held by a community of actors" (Finnemore 1996a: 22).[10] In this regard, the assertions by Ludovico Incisa di Camerana on the immobilism of the Italian foreign policy are revealing (Garruccio 1982: 7–8):

> The two decades between 1961 and 1981 are characterized by the transformation of traditional international factors and the emergence of new factors. The triumph and decline of bipolarism, the ups and downs in the European integration process, the emergence of a strategic polycentrism, accompanied by the dispersion of power and a tendency towards ideological pluralism on a global scale, the end of colonialism and the appearance of a North-South antagonism, are the most significant phenomena in a period that appears extremely more complex than the previous 1947–1960 period, that replaced the alliances forged during World War II with the simpler dichotomy of the Cold War [. . .] Compared with the foreign policy of other countries (France and even West Germany), Italy's foreign policy features an extraordinary degree of regularity and continuity throughout the period [. . .] The regularity

and continuity of Italy's foreign policy can be explained only on the basis of the substantial underlying unity of the Italian political culture with regard to international matters.

Moving on to the explanations based on internal factors, the scholars have highlighted the impact of the peculiar characteristics of Italy's sociopolitical system on its foreign policy, as reflected in the work of both Norman Kogan and Angelo Panebianco.

Kogan argues that the key objective of Italian foreign policy was to defend the domestic social structure from internal threats (Kogan 1963). NATO membership responded to the need of preventing the penetration of communism, while membership of the European Common Market served the purpose of shoring up the shaky economy and preventing any deviation from the liberal model embraced by the economic and political elites.[11] Building on this idea—namely, that foreign policy is merely one of the instruments used by the political and social elites to further and defend their parochial interests—the author reviews the key actors affecting its formation. They are, in order:

1. The political parties.
2. The Parliament, the Government, and the President of the Republic.
3. The Catholic Church.
4. The pressure groups.
5. The bureaucracy.
6. External forces.

As far as the political parties are concerned, Kogan shows how the major contrasts concerning international politics stemmed not so much from any actual differences in the approach to be followed to secure national interest, as from the need to use foreign policy as a form of currency to spend on the domestic coalition market. In other words, the political parties used international issues as a means for accrediting themselves as possible allies of the dominant party.

The institutional actors—the Parliament, the Government, and the President of the Republic—displayed a differing degree of interest in international affairs. Generally speaking, members of Parliament were scarcely interested in foreign policy, save for a few exceptions. The same goes for the government, where, due to its collegial decision-making structure, foreign policy was the result of continual mediation among cabinet members who often supported different policy lines, even within the same political party. In several cases, as in the case of Giovanni Gronchi, the President of the Republic could play an active role, causing quite a few problems to the official line of the government.

Regarding the Catholic Church, Kogan identified different foreign policy visions, some more favorable to the international détente with the

Socialist bloc, out of concern for the vulnerable position of the East European churches, others more favorable to a strategy of hard line confrontation with the USSR. Ultimately, however, the Catholic Church was interested, first and foremost, in preserving its internal power base. This is why it rekindled East-West confrontation issues and the Communist threat whenever needed, especially in connection with domestic elections.

The key lesson that emerges from Kogan's analysis is that Italian political and societal actors are driven by parochial interest and shows little concern for international issues, which are taken into account primarily in connection with the opportunities and threats posed to their respective power positions.[12]

Panebianco has analyzed the impact of domestic politics on foreign policy in a series of articles in which he underlines how Italy's foreign policy was characterized by a low profile, as a result of the dynamics of the political party system and the country's social structure (Panebianco 1977; 1982). Foreign policy, like other public intervention and social regulation tools, is used by governments not only to pursue certain interests in the international arena but also to strengthen or defend their stability. "This means that, like domestic politics, foreign policy depends on the more immediate interests of survival and/or internal consolidation of the political governing elites; it is, therefore, a function of the power struggles within the various States" (Panebianco 1982: 16).[13]

According to Panebianco, once the key decisions to join NATO and the European Community had been taken, Italian politics settled down to a low profile and continued in this approach, without too many jolts, for many years. This passive attitude can be observed in all the strategic areas in which Italy has operated: the Atlantic Alliance, Europe, and the Third World. Regarding the Atlantic Alliance, after joining NATO, Italy's foreign policy featured total subordination to the United States, with practically no significant national initiatives. Likewise, in the case of Europe, Italy was one of the most enthusiastic supporters of the European integration project, wrapping its support with a resounding rhetoric, while failing to contribute any significant ideas and proposals and always transposing the Community directives into national law belatedly and reluctantly. Finally, regarding the developing countries, Rome proved consistently unable to craft a far-reaching strategic plan despite the importance of these areas for the country's energy interests.[14]

Panebianco claims that the reasons for this low profile can be found in the manner the relations between the State and society developed after World War II and in the characteristics of the country's political system.[15] In the postwar period, the Italian State institutions were strongly permeated by social interests. This process is exemplified by formulas such as: "a mix of State-dominated and Stateless society"; "a State-centric model with a weak center"; "lack of State."[16] The weakness of the Italian

State meant that it could easily fall "prey" to private interests, with an unhealthy mingling of public and private actions. "Private interests mix with public interests, creating complex networks where it is difficult to distinguish between the dictates of the State and the requests of private groups, categories, and organizations" (Cassese 1998: 67).

There are multiple causes for the weakness of the Italian State (Panebianco 1982: 18–19):

1. Lack of legitimacy of the concept of nation, as a result of the nationalist excesses of the Fascist period.
2. Weakness of the public administration, both in its civil and military components.
3. Occupation of the State by the political parties, with the emergence of an extreme form of party government.[17]
4. Weakness of the government with respect to the parliament, and ensuing incapacity to formulate clear and effective guidelines.

This first group of causes is integrated by a second group related to how the party system operates. In particular, Panebianco focuses on three key elements:

1. The existence of a dominant party constantly at the center of the political system.
2. The presence of a strong opposition party with antisystem attitudes and a neutralist foreign policy, in contrast with Italy's international position.
3. A political tendency to favor inclusive and "transformist" coalitions, rather than to foster a clear distinction between the majority and the opposition.

The polarization of political party dynamics has supposedly favored the depoliticization of international issues and their removal from the arena of competition for power. By pursuing a passive foreign policy, it could be possible to prevent the international policy divisions from causing further internal fractures, thus exacerbating the already heated public debate. "The depoliticization of foreign policy produced all the 'evils' that observers have always denounced (inefficiency, unpreparedness, lack of political projects, etc.), and that were and remain the price that the political establishment inevitably had to pay—and which it willingly paid—to ensure its self-reproduction and maintain its delicate internal balance" (Ibid.: 19).

Panebianco has once again tackled the same issues in a book on the relationship between democracy and power politics (1997: ch. 10). Comparing Italy with the other European democracies, he observes a strong discrepancy in the Cold War period, resulting in the fact that the other democracies (the United States, the UK, and France) are "warrior democracies," that is, countries prepared to defend and further their national interest even with the use of force, if necessary. Italy, instead, always tended to choose the option of lower international/military profile. Having to choose between spending for welfare or for the military, it consistently preferred the former option. When coming to choose between the forceful pursuit of the national interest and satisfying all political opinions, it preferred the latter option, according to a strategy that privileged the search for the least common denominator.[18] Lastly, in the choice between a nationalist or an internationalist approach, it opted for the latter, subordinating its foreign policy to a multilateral framework.

The analysis by Stefano Silvestri is not too dissimilar. He singles out, from among the factors that contribute to producing a fragmented security policy (with scarce coordination between the military, diplomatic and economic components), a series of characteristics of the political decision-making system (Silvestri 1990: 188–89):

- The presence of coalition governments compelled to mediate between the different political parties composing them.
- The weakness of governments with respect to the parliament, leading to the adoption of policies based on the search for consensus rather than on a clear distinction between the majority and the opposition.
- The presence of the Communist factor.
- The tendency to co-opt the opposition parties.[19]

In the post–Cold War period, there are many studies on the domestic influences on Italy's foreign policy (Pirani 2004: 9–15). Despite the transformations in the political system, many of the elements characterizing the foreign policy in the previous period continued to weigh. In his book on the foreign policies of the EU Member States, Ben Soetendorp highlights how the characteristics of the Italian political system—with a centralized power structure and an uncoordinated political decision-making system—negatively affect the capacity of the country to play an active role in the EU institutions and effectively defend its interests (Soetendorp 1999: ch. 4). Studying the decision-making structure in the field of the security policy, Giuseppe Dottori and Piero Laporta highlight how the Prime Minister's Office, and the Cabinet itself, function like arenas for mediating between the different policy lines already autonomously defined by the single departments, rather than as forums for the definition of general guidelines. "Even key ministers for national security have been affected by this process, operating in an increasingly independent manner" (Dottori, Laporta 1995: 112). The consequences are that the left hand doesn't know what the right hand is doing, a difficult coordination between the foreign and defense policies, and political paralysis if the Ministry of Foreign Affairs and the Ministry of Defense are headed by strong leaders.[20]

The problem of indeterminacy ascribed to the external explanations is found also in the internal explanations that fail to adequately take into account the normative-ideational dimension of political decision. As we will see in chapter 3, examining the works on the military doctrine of the French Army between the two World Wars, the manner in which the bureaucracies responsible for managing security policies react to stimuli from the domestic political dynamics is influenced by the organizational subcultures that limits the repertoire of strategies to be followed (Kier 1996).

The literature examined in part one shows how the domestic and international material factors alone are insufficient to explain foreign policy decisions. We need to consider the belief systems shared by the leaders of a country, through which these elements are viewed and interpreted. In particular, with regard to security we need to understand the strategic culture of a country: the historically sedimented attitude towards war and the use of force. The way in which a country responds to threats, in terms of *realpolitik* practices or conciliatory strategies, are culturally acquired through processes of socialization and institutionalization and not automatically imposed by the logic of international anarchy or by internal political compromises that can produce very different solutions.

BOOK ORGANIZATION

The book consists of two parts. In part one (chapters 2 and 3), I examine the sociological turn in international relations and the emergence of the studies on strategic cultures. Part two (chapters 4 and 5) is dedicated to the study of Italy's strategic cultures and foreign policy.

Chapter 2 describes several of the principal sociological contributions to the analysis of international relations. Two particularly interesting approaches have been identified with regard to the analysis of foreign policy: constructivism and sociological institutionalism. Constructivism highlights the role played by ideational factors. It underlines the social nature of international structures, that is, the role played by the way in which policy makers define themselves and perceive others, developing identities and preferences and behaving accordingly. Sociological institutionalism studies social behavior in terms of role expectations rather than of rational means/ends calculations. It focuses on the processes of institutional imitation and learning. These two approaches give rise to several research projects: the study of security cultures, which focuses on the ideational bases of States' decisions about the use of force and the management of external threats; and the analysis of the learning processes in foreign policy, which investigates the manner in which the States learn to implement practices based on *realpolitik* or nonviolent negotiation strategies. At the end of the chapter there is an overview of how the study of security cultures—of which the strategic cultures are a component—can represent a theoretical bridge linking the various research lines.

Chapter 3 contains an in-depth review of the literature on strategic cultures, describing the different waves of studies since the end of World War II, and the methodological differences between the various works. At the end of the chapter, the research method used to study the Italian strategic cultures is outlined.

After having established the theoretical coordinates, I reconstruct the characteristics of the Italian strategic culture, and how they have influenced the country's international behavior, with special focus on the attitude towards military conflicts and the use of force. Chapter 4 describes the characteristics of the strategic culture of Republican Italy—comparing it with that of the Liberal and Fascist periods—and the causes leading to its formation. Finally, chapter 5 tries to show the impact of this strategic culture on the security policy, analyzing the behavior in militarized interstate disputes, the defense expenditure trends, the support for international organizations and the salient features of the principal military interventions in which Italy has taken part in the post–Cold War period.

The conclusions summarize the empirical evidence emerged from the analysis.

NOTES

1. It should not be forgotten that, for a certain period, Italy also contemplated the idea of developing its own nuclear deterrent, for which it had the necessary financial, technological, and industrial resources (Albonetti 1998).

2. The liberal and neoliberal theories of international relations should not be confused. The former, represented in the work by Moravcsik (1997) and the studies on bureaucratic politics (Allison 1971; Halperin 1974), focus on the negotiations at national level between the various governmental organizations and social actors and their impact on foreign policy decisions. The latter, exemplified in the work by Keohane and Nye (1989), focus on the effects of economic interdependence and of international institutions.

3. For an introduction to the Italian post-WWII foreign policy, see Graziano (1968), Ronzitti (1977), Santoro (1991), Bosworth, and Romano (1991), Gaja (1995), Ferraris (1996), Varsori (1998), Coralluzzo (2000), Romano (2002), Mammarella, Cacace (2008).

4. The so-called Historical Compromise strategy was born of the awareness, by Enrico Berlinguer, that the United States would never have allowed the PCI to take power after winning an election (Olivi 1978).

5. The importance assigned by Santoro to the geographical factor is summed up in the phrase: "Geography, therefore, influences foreign policy today more than we could have expected as a result of the evolution of technology, the means of communication, and of the economic development" (Santoro 1991: 70).

6. Regarding the influence of geographical factors on the Italian foreign policy, see also Jean (1995: ch. 10), who offers a geopolitical interpretation.

7. See the illustration on the cover of the book edited by Bosworth and Romano (1991).

8. "Italy, historically the latest power to emerge on the European scene—because, since the time of Frederick the Great, Prussia was already a great power long before the creation of the German Empire—also ranked last demographically, economically

and militarily. It was considered as a 'great power' only in name and form, rather than in fact" (Chabod 1965: 563).

9. For a detailed review of Italy's contribution to international security in the post–Cold War period, see Foradori, Rosa (2010).

10. See chapter 2 for a more detailed analysis of these issues.

11. "In spite of some mixed feelings about the private business sector, since the war, the DC has attempted to foster what might be called a 'neo-liberal' economic climate" (Posner 1977: 816)

12. Kogan begins his research with an analysis of the characteristics of Italian society, inspired by the well-known study by Edward Banfield on amoral familism (1967). The Italian lack of interest in foreign policy issues, and in public issues in general, would spring from this basic attitude.

13. Charles Yost writes (1972: 22): "The overriding objective of most governments is, of course, to stay in power. They therefore must pursue a foreign policy which is at least tolerable to the politically active part of the population, which can be a small elite in a totalitarian State or the majority of the electorate in a democracy." One of the scholars who has focused most on this topic is Joe Hagan (1995). He identifies two domestic imperatives that influence the international policy decisions of a country. Every politician is concerned with two domestic political imperatives: building policy coalitions that support his program, and to maintain political power. These two imperatives can be achieved through three strategies. A strategy of isolating foreign policy from domestic politics. A mobilization strategy, with the effect of boosting an assertive foreign policy: governments are inclined to take many risks and commitments in order to divert public attention from domestic problems. A strategy of accommodation between the different domestic actors involved, in an attempt to reach a compromise acceptable to everyone. This strategy has a depressive effect on foreign policy and is conducive to adopting a low profile. This is the case with Italy.

14. The only exception to this situation being the attempt made by Enrico Mattei to conduct an independent foreign policy based on the "energy weapon."

15. On the influence of this factor, see also Posner (1977) and Rosa (2006).

16. These definitions are taken from Sabino Cassese (1998: 17–18).

17. According to Pasquino (2002: 17), the peculiarity of Italy, compared to other European experiences, is that the number of institutional and economic positions occupied by persons linked to the political parties is much higher in Italy than in other countries, such as Britain, Germany, or France. Furthermore, in Italy, tenure in these positions is much longer; alternation of positions is less frequent and in some cases the incumbents remain indefinitely in certain positions. A second distinctive feature of party government in Italy is that, thanks to the presence of a widespread clientelistic network with social actors who benefit from a close relationship with politics, governing parties have had to worry less about any assessment by the electorate.

18. Emblematic, in this regard, are the foreign policy difficulties encountered by the coalition governments headed by Romano Prodi.

19. Valter Coralluzzo also highlights how domestic factors have complicated Italy's search for a clear international position. He claims, in fact, that one of the factors that have "caused this indeterminate status, that is, the gap between 'rank and role' mentioned above, is the excessive propensity of the foreign policy to being conditioned by the competition between the political parties" (Coralluzzo 2000: 368).

20. Regarding this issue, see the analysis of the Airbus A400M case that broke out in 2001. It highlights the political and bureaucratic conflicts between the Ministry of Foreign Affairs, the Ministry of Defense, and economic actors, with the Prime Minister's Office playing an entirely passive role (Rosa 2006: 137–42).

I

The Study of Strategic Culture in International Relations

TWO

The Sociological Turn in International Relations

In the last twenty years there has been significant change in the study of international relations, with the emergence of a growing interest in theories and concepts taken from sociology. This was provoked by the theoretical shortcomings present in the explanations of the end of the Cold War by the dominant approaches: neorealism and neoliberalism. The explicative weaknesses of these approaches largely derive from the fact that they underestimate the domestic dynamics of the States, particularly regarding the role played by the change of ideas of the leaders about international politics.[1] The sociological turn stemmed from the confluence of two theoretical movements, the first putting the State at the center of analysis,[2] the second interested in revaluating the weight of cultural factors in the explanation of international relations.[3] The theoretical reorientation has lead to greater focus on the way the characteristics of society influence external behavior. Two approaches are described in this chapter—social constructivism and sociological institutionalism—that put ideational and normative factors and their influence on international decisions at the center of theoretical reflection. Two research projects derive from these two approaches: the study of security cultures and the analysis of the relationship between learning processes and foreign policy.

CONSTRUCTIVISM

The constructivist approach,[4] according to Alexander Wendt, is based on two assumptions: social structures are made up of ideas and not of material elements; and the identity and the interests of the actors are influenced by these social structures. Thus, constructivism can be seen as a sort of "structural idealism" (Wendt 1999: 1).

Wendt's constructivism is State-centric as are neorealism and neoliberalism.[5] It differentiates from these approaches in its rejection of the exogenous concept of national interests. According to the constructivist approach, States do not interact based on preformed identities and interests. It is in the interaction process itself that the identities are constituted and social preferences are formulated. Through this process, the identities and interests are continually reproduced, giving life to social structures, namely the consolidation of a system of expectations regarding one's own role and the other actors. During the interaction process the identities and interests can vary, bringing about changes in the international system.

The importance that Wendt assigns to the processes, in addition to the structures, is another element of differentiation from the mainstream concepts, and especially from Waltz's neorealism. Waltz takes into consideration as an explicative variable only the structure of the international system, conceiving it materialistically, that is, as the result of the distribution of power and resources. For Wendt, international structures are essentially social phenomena. They are determined by the way in which the States perceive one another and by the mutual expectations formed on their behaviors. He distinguishes three types of international structure, which he calls "cultures of anarchy." With this expression he means that anarchy—considered to be a central point by neorealism and neoliberalism to explain international behaviors—cannot be studied as a unitary phenomenon that always generates the same types of stimuli. There are different forms of anarchy producing different kinds of State behaviors. He distinguishes three cultures of anarchy, depending on the type of prevalent roles and identities: the Hobbesian culture; the Lockean culture; the Kantian culture.

The Hobbesian culture of anarchy is characterized by the fact that States consider themselves as enemies. In a Hobbesian type of anarchy system, the States interpret international politics as a zero-sum game, as a struggle for survival: the other State is an enemy that must be destroyed in order to safeguard one's own security. According to Wendt, this type of logic, marked by a war of all against all, has often been dominant over the years and still is today in many parts of the world. The latest centuries, however, have been characterized mainly by the Lockean culture of anarchy.

The Lockean culture of anarchy asserted itself with the constitution of the Westphalian State system, in which the main actors no longer consider themselves as enemies but as rivals. The difference between an enemy and a rival is essentially tied to the emergence of the idea of sovereignty: even if there can be deep contrasts between States and heated conflicts, the States acknowledge the mutual right to exist, the absolute authority of a government in its own internal affairs and its autonomy in conducting its foreign policy. The States can clash, but they avoid trying to eliminate one another. The prevalence of the Lockean culture of anarchy, according to Wendt, explains the low "mortality rate" of States in the last few centuries.

Finally, the third type of culture of anarchy is the Kantian one, which has not fully established itself but is nonetheless present in some international subsystems, such as the Transatlantic system. In an international system where the Kantian culture of anarchy prevails, the actors consider each other as friends: they solve disputes using pacific means and are willing to help each other whenever the security of one of them is threatened by external sources.

International political change, which represents a thorn in the side of the neorealist and neoliberal theories, is seen by Wendt as the passage from one type of culture of anarchy to another. The transition from a Lockean culture to a Kantian culture implies the development of a collective identity among the States, that is, the identification between the State's own interest and the interest of the fellow State. Four factors can promote this development: interdependence; a common destiny; homogeneity; and self-restraint (the latter condition is necessary, but not sufficient, for the other three factors to have a positive impact on the relations between States).

Interdependence can encourage States to cooperate and lead to the development of a collective identity in the long run. In situations of interdependence, there is always the risk that someone takes advantage of the situation to favor himself to the detriment of the others, so it is necessary that interdependence be backed up by a tendency towards self-restraint. The "common destiny" factor refers to those situations in which the well-being and security of a State depend on what happens to the entire group it belongs to. The presence of a threat can drive the States to form alliances. The participation in a group can, however, bring with it the fear of being exploited by the others. So in this case as well, it is important that the States follow rules of self-restraint. Finally the "homogeneity" factor, that produces an agreement on values and institutions, can attenuate the causes of conflict and facilitate the development of a collective identity.

Security Cultures and Foreign Policy

When speaking of constructivism, the research tradition centering on security cultures is of particular interest for foreign policy analysis. The study of security cultures tends to show how the attitude of the States towards the issues regarding threats and the use of force is not necessarily determined by the material conditions of the international system (anarchy and distribution of power) but is influenced by ideational factors (rules of behavior, belief systems) which encourage policy-makers to interpret the events differently and to adopt particular strategies.

The fact that a State follows a *realpolitik* strategy to reach its international objectives does not derive so much from imperatives attributable to the pressure exerted by the structure of the international system, as from the fact that the leaders of the country have understood and internalized a realist security culture. They have developed an attitude, an image of international politics leading them to privilege the military approach, to emphasize the importance of the nation's power, and so forth. This is where Iain Johnston's (1995b) expression "cultural realism" as opposed to Kenneth Waltz's expression "structural realism" (1979) comes from: the first indicates that realism is a culturally learned behavior model; the second, that it is an adaptive behavior imposed by the characteristics of the international system.

The study of security cultures and their impact on the States' foreign policies is at the center of Peter Katzenstein's work (1996a). The starting point of his reflection is that the preferences of the States and their behavior are determined culturally. This explains why States, when facing similar situations, choose to respond differently: with military or diplomatic solutions, defensive or offensive strategies.

The decision to study the traditional issues of national security stems from the will to challenge the neorealist models on what is their ideal ground, regarding which they would seem to offer strong and parsimonious explanations. This is the same research strategy used by Graham Allison (1971) to demonstrate the limits of the explanation models based on the rational actor paradigm. He concentrates on the international crises because in these situations the political and bureaucratic division between policy-makers inevitably tends to be relegated to second place. Therefore, if even in these extreme cases we discover that it is impossible to offer reliable explanations without recalling the social aspects of the decision-making process, that is, the different nature of the actors involved and of the interests they promote (which influence their way of looking at an issue and the strategies proposed to address it), all the more so this should be true in those situations in which the centripetal tendencies of the decision-making process are less accentuated. This is a "hard test" strategy: to compare a theoretical model with an empirical case which, by its very nature, can be better explained using competing approaches. Along this line, Katzenstein (1996b: 11) writes:

> This book deals with what most scholars of national security would consider to be hard cases. It chooses political topics and empirical domains that favor well-established perspectives in the field of national security. If the style of analysis and the illustrative case material can establish plausibility here, it should be relatively easy to apply this book's analytical perspective to broader conceptions of security that are not restricted to military issues or to the state.

Katzenstein singles out two ideational elements affecting the foreign policies of the States: the cultural-institutional context and the political identities. The first element refers to all the norms, procedures, principles and rules influencing the behavior of the political actors. The different political and organizational cultures of France and of Japan condition their foreign policy-making process. The French organizational culture favors the centralization and verticalization of the decision-making process in the field of security, in which the figure of the president dominates. The Japanese culture, with its emphasis on hierarchy and its respect of the principle of seniority, produces a political system dominated by the upper levels of the ruling class. At the same time, the search for the consent of the largest possible number of people determines a decision-making style encouraging the dispersion of information and a continuous negotiation (Sampson 1987).

The second element refers to the way in which the States define themselves and how identities are formed through interaction with the others and the pressures of internal dynamics. The military defeat of Germany, Japan, and Italy in World War II played a fundamental role in the emergence of a "pacifist" political identity. As concerns Italy, the strong presence of left-wing and Catholic political groups, both promoters of a vision of refusal of war as a political instrument, contributed in shaping its strategic culture.

The shaping of identities determines the development of specific preferences. A country that considers itself as a trading (or pacifist) State will act differently than one identifying itself as a military superpower. National interests are not considered as an exogenous variable but as part of the model: as an element to be explained and not an assumption. The interests pursued by the States through their foreign policy can change as social identities change, which in turn change as a consequence of the interaction with other States.

The cultural factors provide the "lenses" through which international events are interpreted and the response strategies are processed. There are five processes through which cultural factors shape security policies (Jepperson, Wendt, Katzenstein 1996: 52):

1. Cultural and institutional elements directly influence the national interests and the security policies of the States. The refusal of some States to contemplate the use of force as a viable political option directly affects the level of military expense, the format of the Armed Forces, and the tendency to militarize the security issues.
2. Cultural and institutional elements influence the identities of States. In this case the cultural influence is indirect, because it is mediated by the development of a social identity affecting the State's preferences and foreign policy.

3. Changes of identities influence national interests. The transition of Japan from a military, expansionist State to a trading State after World War II is a case in point.
4. State identities influence international structures. This is what Wendt refers to when he mentions the culture of anarchy, asserting that the different structures of the international systems are essentially defined by the intersubjective meaning attributed to them, more than by the distribution of the material power factors. The latter assume a precise meaning only with reference to the prevalent culture: in the European-Western subsystem, characterized by a Kantian-type culture, the presence of a neighbor disposing of nuclear weapons assumes an entirely different meaning than the same situation in the Middle East or Southern Asia, where a Hobbesian culture prevails.
5. The behavior of the States contributes to building and reproducing international structures. Anarchy is not an inevitable condition in the relational life of nations, but rather the result of repeated actions of the States that with their behavior, based on mistrust and prudence, contribute to the generation of the security dilemma.[6]

SOCIOLOGICAL INSTITUTIONALISM

Social constructivism and sociological institutionalism are not easily distinguishable, since they are actually simply two faces of the same coin. They are discussed here separately only for convenience, to state more clearly the explicative aspects they respectively focus on.

Martha Finnemore (1996b) believes that it is useful to import sociological institutionalism into the study of international relations for many reasons:

1. First of all it provides an efficient challenge to the dominant paradigms: neorealism and neoliberalism. It makes it possible to formulate theories that can be controlled empirically regarding the impact of cultural factors on the international behavior of the States.
2. Second, sociological institutionalism—by putting the development of international rules and their diffusion process at the center of the analysis—makes it possible to establish fruitful theoretical contacts with other approaches, such as the English school and the studies on globalization.
3. Even though sociological institutionalism has much in common with constructivism, according to Finnemore it provides deeper and more detailed explanations, thanks to a better understanding of social structures. Moreover, sociology emphasizes how the insti-

tutions, intended as rules of behavior, are pervasive of every aspect of social life and not only of the political domain.
4. Fourth, sociological institutionalism puts great attention on the historical dimension, and thus considers the temporal evolution of the social institutions as something to be explained and not an assumed element. States are influenced by the norms and ideas that are prevalent in a given era.
5. Finally, sociological institutionalism makes it possible to counter impressive images, such as the image of a clash of civilizations, fomenting alternate theories on cultural homogenization phenomena.

Some interesting lines of research derive from these elements. The concept of institutional imitation makes it possible to explain the worldwide spread of the State organizational form, though it often proves to be inefficient in performing its functions (providing for the well-being or the security of its citizens).[7] Since the Western State is considered as a form of "modern" political organization and benefits from wide international legitimization, it follows that all the other States desiring to obtain the same recognition tend to a similar political structure. "[. . .] virtually all states have defense ministries even when they face no external threat. Further, virtually all states have tripartite military structures, with an army, air force, and navy—even landlocked states" (Ibid.: 336–37). In the same way, if nuclear weapons are considered as a symbol of international rank, all States will try to acquire them, notwithstanding their practical utility.

An essential point of sociological institutionalism is that people do not behave according to a utilitarian logic, continuously comparing costs and benefits and choosing the most efficient line of conduct, but they conform to the expectations of the reference groups. People tend to behave congruously with the position they occupy, following the expectations the others have for them. This is called the logic of appropriateness, as opposed to the logic of consequentiality. The institutions provide the basic criteria for judging the appropriateness of the actions carried out (March, Olsen 1989).

The importance attributed to the appropriate rather than to the efficient behavior implies that a State may follow a line of conduct which does not appear to be rationale from a strictly realistic standpoint, which prescribes a line of conduct pursuing the maximization of security or power at all times. According to Scott Sagan, Ukraine's choice to dispose of the nuclear arsenal it inherited in the wake of the dissolution of the Soviet Union was mainly determined by the weight the international regime assigned to nonproliferation policies as a symbol of responsible power.

The strength of the NPT regime created a history in which the most recent examples of new or potential nuclear states were so-called "rogue states" such as North Korea, Iran and Iraq. This was hardly a nuclear club whose new members would receive international prestige, and during the debate in Kiev, numerous pro-NPT Ukrainian officials insisted that renunciation of nuclear weapons was now the best route to enhance Ukraine's international standing (Sagan 1996/1997: 81).

Learning and Foreign Policy

Interest in the rules of behavior leads to the study of which appropriateness criteria the policy-makers managing foreign policy learn and in which way, i.e., through which historical experiences and interactions with others.

John Vasquez stresses the role of historical experience in foreign policy learning processes. According to Vasquez, the coming to power of people belonging to different social generations affects the management of foreign policy (Vasquez 1985). The changes of direction in a country's strategy are seen as the consequence of the succession of generations of leaders learning different lessons from history (May, Neustadt 1986). In the field of foreign policy, great world events such as crises, wars, and revolutions play a decisive role in the formation of a generation. People whose personal experience has been influenced by these events will develop particular belief systems and will interpret world events according to the lessons learned from the past. Power policies and compromise strategies are practices that are learned culturally by the leaders of a country. The problem is to understand which are the social and political conditions that determine the emergence of promoters of choices fostering the use of force or supporters of pacific means of intervention.

The explicative variables considered by Vasquez are the prevalent opinion on the utility of the last war fought and its outcome. If it is deemed that it was right to bear the costs of a war, "hawk" leaders, supporters of *realpolitik* practices, will tend to emerge. The supporters of a confrontational policy, the hard-liners, besides showing a behavior favorable to an aggressive foreign policy and the use of military force, have a greater inclination to taking risks and, on the psychological level, show a poorer cognitive complexity. They depict the world in a stereotyped manner and consider violence as a simple, quick way to solve international problems. They tend to be more frequently subject to militaristic and nationalistic attitudes and this makes them more inclined to engage in power politics and aggressive behaviors (Vasquez 1993).

Conversely, when the utility of the war fought is judged negatively, in the political elite the supporters of a compromise-oriented political line (accommodationists*)* will prevail. The accommodationists tend to reject the use of war as a legitimate and efficient instrument of foreign policy, preferring the use of negotiation, compromise, and international institutions to solve conflicts. They tend to avoid risky actions and do not take useless risks. Their cognitive map is complex and sophisticated and consequently they reject the idea that the use of force can represent a valid shortcut. Therefore they are less inclined to be dragged along into power politics dynamics.

The second variable, victory or defeat in the last war fought, determines the degree of stability of the political elite: the homogeneity of the security culture and the presence or absence of internal opposition. By crossing the two variables, four types of leadership emerge (stable hardliners, instable hard-liners, stable accommodationists, and instable accommodationists). If the costs borne are considered acceptable and the outcome of the war was victory, we will have a generation of hawks firmly in command. If the costs are considered unacceptable and the outcome of the war was defeat, the ruling class will be made up by doves who will not meet with very much resistance from the rest of society or the political class. In the other two cases (useless victory or useful defeat), ruling classes with weak convictions, competing strategic subcultures, and strong political contrasts will emerge.

Iain Johnston (2008), too, concentrates on the learning processes in foreign policy behavior, but rather than dealing with the consequences of significant historical events such as wars, he analyzes the socialization effects produced by the participation in international institutions. He observes the growing participation of Chinese diplomats in multilateral organizations concerned with arms control, trying to demonstrate how this has attenuated their inclination towards *realpolitik* attitudes. He singles out three learning processes: mimicking, social influence, and persuasion.[8]

When entering into a group for the first time, people tend to imitate its behavior, passively adopting its rules, procedures, and linguistic forms. Initially it is not clear what the benefits and costs deriving from participation will be, so it is more prudent to conform to the values of the group, if only superficially. In comparison with the other two socialization mechanisms, the imitation processes do not entail the internalization of new rules and the modification of one's own preferences. It is a behavior dictated by an attempt to survive in a situation of uncertainty. Nonconforming behaviors, if repeated over time, even if they do not trigger penalizing reactions, could prevent the actor from receiving the benefits from participating in the group.

At domestic level, mimicking processes produce three effects. The first consists of the creation of organizations in charge of the management of matters dealt with by the institutions a country is participating in. This results in the emergence of a political and bureaucratic constituency that is interested in continuing the interaction with the institution because its very existence depends on this.

The second effect consists of the fact that the organizations managing the relationships with an institution must train their personnel to master new techniques, new behavior models, and new standard operating methods if they want to be efficient.

The third aspect concerns the adoption of the discourse practices prevalent in the institution. All organizations develop their own way of expressing a political discourse, indicating what themes are or are not acceptable, which arguments can be used and which arguments are considered to be inappropriate. State officials, who on the international level adopt the discourse practices of the institutions they participate in, tend to reproduce these practices on the domestic level. The result is that a certain way of speaking and thinking about foreign policy also spreads to the national level.

The second socialization mechanism, based on social influence, works at a deeper level, bringing about a change in the identity of the actor (Ibid.: ch. 3). This is based on the fact that people desire to obtain not only a concrete gain, but also a social reward from belonging to a group. The need for personal acceptance is as important as material advantages. People seek the recognition of their peers and want to avoid their disapproval. This process comes from the fact that a person who has internalized the values of a group attributes importance to its judgement regarding his conduct. He is no longer an occasional participant, but a full-fledged member. Once a sense of belonging to the *in-group* has been developed, he will tend to assume attitudes and behaviors that are congruent with the logic of appropriateness defined by the group members. Social influence mechanisms act in different ways. At the root of each of these mechanisms is the desire to improve one's own status. In order to accumulate symbolic "status markers," whether through praise, back-patting, and so forth, people tend to behave in a manner consistent with the expectations regarding the line of conduct to be followed in a given situation, considering the identity they bear.

The third socialization mechanism, persuasion, brings about a change in personal beliefs (Ibid.: ch. 4). Through social interaction, dialogue, contacts, and reasoning, there is a change in ideas about certain subjects: environment, armament control, nuclear proliferation, economy, human rights, etc. In this case, complex learning processes take place: the actors modify their own causal beliefs—what the effects of certain actions are— and their own concept of national interest (Levy 1994). For example, the official of a country participating in a multilateral debate over arms control could convince himself that his country's behavior, contrary to this type of measure, can be a source of international instability rather than security; that certain measures implying the assessment of treaty compliance by independent agencies (such as IAEA) do not represent intrusion in the domestic matters of a country but useful instruments for building a climate of trust; that national interest can be better pursued through transparency policies rather than through policies aiming at deceiving the opponent.

THE STUDY OF SECURITY CULTURES AS A THEORETICAL "BRIDGE"

The two lines of research described above ("security cultures" and "learning and foreign policy"), besides sharing a common sociological origin, also share a high potential for integration, in that they do not merely represent alternative explanations but they reinforce and support each other in producing significant analysis.

There is a close connection between the study of security cultures and of learning processes. The latter explain where the country's security cultures come from and what national and international events determine their changes. This fact opens a fruitful collaboration with historical sociology.[9] As security cultures develop in the course of a historical process, they require a diachronic analysis.[10] In the same way, dramatic historical events can cause changes in a country's security culture.

Security cultures are learned through socialization processes. Analyzing the daily practices by which they are spread—by, for example, the work of the epistemic communities (Haas 1992)[11]—or the historical international events affecting an entire generation of decision-makers, is a way of emphasizing the close connection between the two traditions of study. The concept of security culture, going back to the idea of a learned international behavior, requires an in-depth analysis of the way these ideas are selected and transmitted, and of the way they continue over time or are replaced by new ones.

The next chapter describes the strategic culture that represents, in the area of security cultures, a line of research strictly focused on problems related to war and to the grand strategy of a country.[12] Strategic cultures condition the framing of events, that is, a conflictual versus a peaceful image of interstate relations, and the reactions of the leaders, that is, the use of negotiation versus the use of force. In the second part, the concept of strategic culture will be used to analyze the Italian case.

NOTES

1. According to Rey Koslowski and Friedrich Kratochwil (1994), the end of the Cold War was determined by the fact that at a certain point Gorbachev and his closest collaborators repudiated the "Brezhnev doctrine" and the use of violent means to ensure the unity of the Empire. This change derived from the elaboration of new ideas regarding international politics and relations with the Western States drawn up by a small group of soviet analysts and policymakers of progressivist orientation. See also Hermann (1996).

2. International relations researchers following the domestic structure approach tend to focus on the State-society relationship. For a comprehensive survey of studies on domestic structure and foreign policy, see Rosa (2006).

3. Studies on the ideational bases of foreign policy and studies on domestic structure have many points in common. Steven Rosen adopts a definition of domestic structure referring to ideational factors. The domestic structure of India, which he studied, centers on a system of beliefs regarding the organization of society in separate castes, tied to cultural elements (Rosen 1995). As Matthew Evangelista (1997: 223) puts it: "much of the recent work in domestic structure has paid particular attention to the interaction between a country's domestic structure and the historically derived normative understandings embodied in its society." The role of cultural norms—as key components of the domestic structure of a country—in differentiating the behavior of the States in the field of security was amply emphasized by Katzenstein (1993; Katzenstein, Okawara 1993). Not coincidentally, many exponents of constructivism also study the relationship between domestic structure and foreign policy: Peter Katzenstein, Michael Barnett, Thomas Risse-Kappen.

4. This part on constructivism is taken from Rosa (2003b).

5. The constructivist approach has several variants, of which Wendt's is only the best known and most ambitious due to his intent to construct a general theory. For a more comprehensive survey of the constructivist approach and its internal formulations, see Checkel (1998).

6. The security dilemma represents "a dilemma with which human societies have had to grapple since the dawn of history. For it stems from a fundamental social constellation [. . .] where groups live alongside each other without being organized into a higher unity. Wherever such anarchic society has existed—and it has existed in most periods of known history on some level—here has arisen what may be called the 'security dilemma' of men, or groups, or their leaders. Groups or individuals living in such a constellation must be, and usually are, concerned about their security from being attacked, subjected, dominated, or annihilated by other groups and individuals. Striving to attain security from such attack, they are driven to acquire more and more power in order to escape the impact of the power of others. This, in turn, renders the others more insecure and compels them to prepare for the worst. Since none can ever feel completely secure in such a world of competing units, power competition ensues, and the vicious circle of security and power accumulation is on" (Herz 1950: 157).

7. On this subject, see the work of John Meyer and his collaborators regarding the international diffusion of the organizational and political model of the State-nation (Meyer et. al. 1997).

8. The following is a summary of Johnston (2008). See also Rosa (2010: § 2.3).

9. As Michael Barnett writes, underlining the exchange relations between historical sociology and constructivism (2002: 105): "[H]istorical sociologists have wrestled with the relationship between production and ideational categories in ways that have successfully avoided charges of economic reductionism, and that have forwarded cultural categories in sophisticated ways." Historical sociology problematizes State entities and tries to understand their evolution over time, unlike neorealism that has a static and atemporal conception of State. Historical sociology shows how the political units composing international systems have changed over the years due to the interaction between internal dynamics (economic structure and class relations) and external dynamics (international systems and wars). The definition of historical sociology by John Hobson (2002: 13) derives from this view: *"a critical approach which refuses to treat the present as an autonomous entity outside of history, but insists on embedding it within a specific socio-temporal place."*

10. On this point see what David Haglund (2009: 23) writes: "Analysts who employ strategic culture as a means of accounting for behavior's impact often turn to historical sociology for guidance."

11. In this regard, see the works by Adler (1992) and Evangelista (1995) on the transnational coalition of experts on weapons control and on the role they played in creating new strategies and spreading new military ideas in the former Soviet Union.

12. On the relationship between different types of culture—political, security, strategic—see comments by John Duffield (1999: 776–77).

THREE
The Study of Strategic Cultures

The approach of States to the use of force is not all the same. Some nations are ready to use military force to address their foreign policy issues, while others privilege the diplomatic approach. Some countries invest heavily in building-up their armed forces while others favor other sectors of public expenditure. The various endowments of resources help in comprehending some of these aspects of military conduct, but fail in providing an adequate explanation since it often happens that countries with the same level of economic development and a comparable international position show quite different models of behavior as concerns the use of force. This is because they have peculiar strategic cultures, that is, different belief systems about the role of war, the image of enemies, the utility of military force.

THE THREE WAVES OF STUDIES: WWII, COLD WAR, POST–COLD WAR

The development of the study of strategic cultures can be broken down into various phases. In this paragraph I describe, adopting the periodization by Michael Desch (1998), the studies on strategic cultures based on the nature of the object analyzed. In the second paragraph I will describe the differences in methodology between the various studies.

Desch distinguishes three waves of studies on the relationship between culture and military behavior. The first wave develops during World War II, the second embraces the whole Cold War period, and the third starts with the end of the Cold War. The first wave includes studies aimed at analyzing the culture and "national character" of the Axis powers (Germany and Japan) in order to understand their manner of combat. A classical work that falls into this category is *The Chrysanthemum and the*

Sword: Patterns of Japanese Culture by Ruth Benedict (2005). Benedict's work was financed by the U.S. Office of War Information with the precise aim of achieving a better knowledge about how a country so culturally different from the United States waged its wars. Benedict writes (Ibid.: 1) that a major problem was comprehending "the nature of the enemy. We had to understand their behavior in order to cope with it." To understand the Japanese attitude towards the use of force it was necessary to study Japan's cultural patterns, that is, the value systems and the beliefs affecting social behavior. The resulting issues were of a very practical nature: how far would the Japanese go before surrendering? How much military pressure would be necessary to achieve the final victory? Would it have been necessary to bomb the Emperor's palace in order to obtain their surrender? Would it have been necessary to attack civilian targets to subdue the resistance of the Armed Forces?

One of the aims of Benedict's research was to "look at the way they [the Japanese] conducted the war itself and see it not for the moment as a military problem but as a cultural problem. In warfare as well as in peace, the Japanese acted in character" (Ibid.: 5). In the second chapter, she analyzes the Japanese attitude towards war, highlighting a whole set of differences vis-à-vis to the cultural traditions of Western countries. Benedict compares the assessment of the world situation made by the Americans and by the Japanese. According to the former, World War II resulted from the aggressiveness of the Axis powers. According to the Japanese, it was the result of the anarchical characteristics of the international system that could have been corrected by setting up a power hierarchy with Japan at the apex. Since the respect for hierarchy is an especially appreciated feature of Japanese culture, Japan was the most qualified to transfer this form of social order to the rest of the world. Japan's ideal was that "all nations were to be one world, fixed in an international hierarchy" (Ibid.: 21).

The focus on the international hierarchy issue was closely linked to the importance in Japanese culture of the idea that every individual has to take his proper place. Benedict writes (*Ibid.*: 43):

> Any attempt to understand the Japanese must begin with their version of what it means to "take one's proper station." Their reliance upon order and hierarchy and our faith in freedom and equality are poles apart and it is hard for us to give hierarchy its just due as a possible social mechanism. Japan's confidence in hierarchy is basic in her whole notion of man's relation to his fellow man and of man's relation to the State [. . .] The Japanese have seen the whole problem of international relations in terms of their version of hierarchy, just as they have seen their internal problems in the same light. For the last decade they have pictured themselves as attaining the apex of that pyramid, and now that this position belongs instead to the Western nations, their view of

hierarchy just as certainly underlies their acceptance of the present dispensation.

This hierarchical vision was formally expressed in various diplomatic documents of the time, from the pact of alliance with Rome and Berlin to the declaration of war against the United States after the attack on Pearl Harbor.[1]

A second feature of Japanese culture that directly affected its way of fighting is the importance it attributes to "spiritual" forces versus material forces. Regarding this point, Benedict explains that this does not mean Tokyo neglected the concrete aspects of military power. In the period prior to the onset of World War II, Japan was one of the world's most militarized countries and invested heavily in armaments. Weapons, however, had a strongly symbolical value. "The difference between Japan and Western nations was not that Japan was careless about material armament. But ships and guns were just the outward show of the undying Japanese Spirit. They were symbols much as the sword of the samurai had been the symbol of his virtue" (Ibid.: 23). This nurtured the idea that it was possible to defeat an economically stronger enemy using strategies of mobilization of the population aimed at showcasing the virtues of the Japanese, that is, obstinacy, skill, and abnegation vis-à-vis the firepower of the enemy. Conversely, the American strategic culture magnified technical innovation as the tool for compensating for the strategic and operational shortcomings of their Armed Forces. This has been defined as "technological optimism" that is accompanied by an "industrial" approach to war, namely emphasis on the capacity to quash the enemy through the mere production of enormous quantities of war material (Luttwak 1984; Mahnken 2009).

Another important aspect of Japan's culture, closely linked to its attitude towards war, is that which relates to the uncertainty generated by the unpredictability of events. According to Benedict, the Japanese were not worried about the intrinsic seriousness of an event—be it an air strike or a military defeat—but about the incapacity to foresee the events.[2] This mental attitude translated into a high level of tolerance in the face of even the worst military downturns, as long as they were predicted by the leaders. The loss of a stronghold, a defeat on the battlefield, an attack on the cities were not sources of worry, as long as the Japanese strategists could show the population that they had already been taken into account.

Another factor that stimulated the Japanese attitude towards war was the idea that "the eyes of the world were upon them." This encouraged Japan to exalt warlike virtues, and to fight on until the end, showing a dignified behavior even when faced with defeat.

A particularly complex figure was that of the emperor. During the feudal period, the emperor did not hold an important position in Japanese political hierarchies. The loyalty of the subjects was focused firstly on their feudal lord and secondly on the supreme military commander. This past weakness led American scholars to believe that the emperor's role was a marginal one. On the contrary, Benedict highlights his centrality and the population's total deference towards him, and thus how he was a source of legitimization of political choices, even the most controversial ones. "Japanese commanders, therefore, were playing on an all but unanimous Japanese veneration [. . .] the militarists used the appeal of loyalty to the Emperor in every possible way" (Benedict 2005: 33).

These cultural traits were common throughout Japanese society. Others concerned only or mainly the Armed Forces. One of these involved the management of troops in battle. Japanese soldiers totally scorned death, and so they rejected any kind of precaution or moderation. Soldiers had to fight until the end because this was believed to be the correct behavior. Logistically speaking, this meant a total lack of hospitals. Simply put, Japanese soldiers were not to allow their capture alive or wounded. While the Americans organized hospital camps on the front lines, on the rear, and back home, the Japanese war machine didn't envisage any of this. Surrender was considered a form of dishonor. This explains why only a small number of Japanese soldiers surrendered to American troops. In many cases, the captured soldiers were made prisoners while unconscious and therefore incapable of fighting unto death or of killing themselves before falling into enemy hands. Benedict provides significant data to this regard (Ibid.: 38–39):

> The Army lived up to the code to such an extent that in the North Burma campaign the proportion of the captured to the dead was 142 to 17,166. That was a ratio of 1:120. And of the 142 in the prison camps, all except a small minority were wounded or unconscious when taken; only a very few had "surrendered" singly or in groups of two or three. In the armies of Occidental nations it is almost a truism that troops cannot stand the death of one-fourth to one-third of their strength without giving up; surrenders run about 4:1. When for the first time in Hollandia, however, any appreciable number of Japanese troops surrandered, the proportion was 1:5 and that was a tremendous advance over the 1:120 of North Burma.

Cultural studies such as Benedict's fell into disuse with the onset of the Cold War. This was mainly due to the advent of nuclear weapons. The nuclear revolution caused the ousting of ideational factors in the explanation of the attitude of States regarding the use of force. "Nuclear weapons were so destructive that they made cultural differences largely irrelevant" (Desch 1998: 145). The theories on deterrence of the Fifties and Sixties assumed a rationalistic and homogeneous conception of American and Russian policy-makers, viewed as similarly occupied in making their threats credible, according to the abstract logic of the game theory (Freedman 1989). The two great problems with deterrence—stability and credibility—both betray this perspective.³ The first problem was addressed by Albert Wohlstetter (1959), who analyzed the incorrect assumptions of the American deterrence policy during the Cold War years. According to Wohlstetter, the problem lies in the fact that the so-called balance of terror, on which the bipolar relationship between the United States and the USSR was based after World War II, was anything but automatic, that is, it was not ensured by the mere possession of nuclear weapons. For two States to become dissuaded from attacking each other, they must have a "second strike capability": their nuclear weapon systems must be capable of surviving a surprise attack of the enemy and of retaliating in a devastating manner on the attacker's territory. If this is not the case, a State may decide to strike first in order to destroy the other State's retaliation capacity. At the same time, the State that considers itself strategically vulnerable may attack first in fear of the other State's paralyzing attack. All this would generate a highly unstable situation in which both actors would be induced to tip the balance.

The second problem is psychological and concerns the capacity to persuade the other party about one's own determination. Considering the high risks that both parties would run in starting a nuclear war, it is not simple to convince an aggressor of the credibility of the threat. The problem is not so much related to the cases of direct deterrence, in which national survival is at risk, as to those of extended deterrence, where one risks nuclear war on one's own territory to defend an ally. Thomas Schelling (1963), using analysis derived from the game theory, states that the best way for a State—or for any actor—to make a commitment credible is to put itself in a condition whereby it cannot act in any manner other than that established by the commitment itself, that is, to adopt a strategy that precludes any options different from the one chosen. The actor must choose a line of conduct with little room to maneuver and must signal to the adversary the binding weight of the commitments made, so that the latter abstains from adopting a given policy simply because it has failed to fully comprehend the weight of the obligation taken.

The early 1970s witnessed an important change in American nuclear strategy regarding target selection, which led to a turning away from the system of mutually assured destruction. The new policy envisaged the opportunity of using nuclear weapons not only as a deterrent tool but also as an instrument to be used in a limited manner for attacks against enemy forces. This revision was supported by the need, more or less acknowledged by all of the governments, to provide the policy-makers with a larger number of practicable options in the event that deterrence failed, as well as to justify the process of nuclear armament modernization. The new strategic line, implemented through memorandum NSDM-242, was first announced in March 1974 during the testimony of Secretary of Defense James Schlesinger before Congress (Cordesman 1982: 14). The core of Schlesinger's policy was the "limited strategic options" concept: part of the atomic arsenal would be used against non-military, low population density targets, and military targets within the Soviet Union and in the territories of its Warsaw Pact allies. The assumption underlying this revision was that the American behavior, aimed at keeping any use of nuclear weapons under control, would be reciprocated by a similar behavior by the Soviets.

In contrast to the theoretical postulates of the Schlesinger doctrine — namely, that the Soviet leaders would act in the same manner as the American policymakers — Jack Snyder published in 1977 with the Rand Corporation a paper on strategic culture. Snyder claimed it was wrong to think that the Soviet leaders would tackle nuclear issues in the same way as the Americans. Soviet leaders should not be thought of as generic abstract actors trying to maximize their profit, according to the formal game theory logic, but "as politicians and bureaucrats who have developed and been socialized into a strategic culture that is in many ways unique and who have exhibited distinctive stylistic predispositions in their past crisis behavior" (Snyder 1977: 4).

Snyder defines strategic culture as the sum of ideas, conditioned emotional responses, and recurring behavior patterns that members of a community have acquired through socialization mechanisms. This set of attitudes and beliefs affects the way in which strategic problems are framed, the debate that accompanies them, and the setting up of actions. By virtue of a strategic culture's resistance to change, people tend to respond to international events in constant ways.

Starting from these considerations, Snyder examines the characteristics of Soviet strategic culture, its origins, and its effect on the Kremlin's attitude towards the use of nuclear weapons. He underlines how one of the key elements of America's post–World War II deterrence policy — namely the acceptance of a system of mutually assured destruction in which none of the contestants can attack and think of getting away with it, due to the certainty of a devastating retaliation — was entirely absent from the strategic thought of the Soviet leaders.

Snyder identifies other differences between Russians and Americans with regard to the notion of limited nuclear war, theorized by analysts such as Henry Kissinger (1957) and Hermann Kahn (1965). In the attitude of the Soviet planners one could observe forms of moderation prior to the use of nuclear weapons, but once this threshold was crossed there would have been no stop to the use of the nuclear arsenal. This position was a far cry from the formulations on the ladders of escalation set forth by American scholars.[4] In short, Soviet policy foresaw no restriction in selecting targets as imagined by the Schlesinger doctrine.

This difference in outlooks derived from a peculiar strategic culture that pushed Moscow to behave differently from Washington when faced with the possibility of war. This distinct strategic culture was the result of the following set of factors:

- The security environment.
- A unique historical experience.
- A political system in which the military played a key role.

The first source of differentiation of the Soviet strategic culture is the peculiarity of its geopolitical position. In the years following World War II, the USSR found itself in a condition of strategic superiority with respect to the United States. in the Old Continent due to the fact that the conventional forces of the Warsaw Pact greatly outnumbered those of NATO. This "conventional imbalance in Europe provides the Soviets with no compelling incentives or requirements to develop a doctrine of limited theater nuclear war" (Ibid.: 23). A second strategic factor that drove Moscow to refuse the possibility of a theatre nuclear war was that the war would have been fought in Europe anyhow, an aspect highly detrimental to Moscow's interests. In fact, what for Washington was a limited war was not the same for the Kremlin. Third, the USSR had invested more than the United States in a system of civil defenses capable of reducing the destructive impact of nuclear weapons. In addition to this, the population and the major industrial centers were disseminated over an immense land. This made the argument about damage limitation less interesting. Fourth, the strategic debate between the civilian executives of the Kremlin and the military favored a unilateral defense strategy scarcely sensitive to America's attempts to reach an agreed position on the possibility of using limited options in the event of a conflict.

As for the historical heritage, World War II and the enormous suffering it caused had made the Soviet population and Soviet leaders capable of withstanding much higher levels of destruction than those to which the Americans were used to.

Finally, unlike the United States, where the main theories regarding the use of nuclear weapons had been conceived by scholars coming from academic circles, in the USSR the military enjoyed a dominating position in this sector. "Historically, the military's monopoly on expertise has extended not only to hardware but also to the elaboration of strategic doctrine. And understandably, their perspective on strategic problems has tended to follow the 'narrow logic of military efficiency'" (Ibid.: 30).

Within the context of strategic culture, there may exist various subcultures linked to special groups, organizations, or institutions. Snyder defines a strategic subculture as follows (Ibid.: 10):

> A strategic subculture will be defined as a subsection of the broader strategic community with reasonably distinct beliefs and attitudes on strategic issues, with a distinct and historically traceable analytical tradition, with characteristic institutional associations, and with more or less distinct patterns of socialization to the norms of the subculture. At

the same time, members of subcultures are also members of the broader strategic culture. Thus, members of distinct subcultures within the general Soviet strategic culture are more likely to share fundamental outlooks with each other than with members of the American strategic culture.

Snyder studied the strategic subcultures of the European General Staffs at the onset of World War I and their impact on the security policies of the great powers that sparked disaster in August 1914.

Interest in the origins of World War I did not stem from historical curiosity but from the preoccupation that a nuclear conflict between the United States and USSR could explode without warning, just like in August 1914 when a whole set of internal and external political conditions—bipolarization of the world into two opposite alliances, rigidity of the military plans, the mobilization trap, an aggressive culture—drove the European powers to make an abysmal decision that none really wanted.

The debate was launched by an article published in *Foreign Affairs* by Miles Kahler (1979–1980) that expressly underlined the similarity between the political situation in the late 1970s and the one previous to the onset of World War I. Through an overview of the characteristics of the international system and of the domestic conditions of the superpowers, he highlighted the similarities between the situations of the two periods and the relating risks. One of the factors deemed potentially hazardous with regard to international stability and the possible onset of war was the offensive mentality of the nuclear strategists of the early 1980s that was reminiscent of that of the military dealing with the July 1914 crisis. The Reagan administration displayed an aggressive nuclear strategy that even included preventive attacks (Gray, Payne 1980). In the balance between defensive and offensive actions, the latter were prevailing.

The "cult of the offensive," that had contributed in precipitating World War I, could be studied in order to understand the risks of the nuclear balance (Van Evera 1984: 106):

> The 1914 case bears directly on the debate about these counterforce strategies,[5] warning that the dangers of counterforce include but also extend far beyond the well-known problems of "crisis instability" and pre-emptive war. If the superpowers achieved disarming counterforce capabilities, or if they believed they had done so, the entire political universe would be disturbed. The logic of self-protection in a counterforce world would compel much of the same behavior and produce the same phenomena that drove the world to war in 1914—dark political and military secrecy, intense competition for resources and allies, yawning windows of opportunity and vulnerability, intense arms-racing, and offensive and preemptive war plans of great scope and violence.

The *cult of the offensive* refers to an attitude of the European elite in the early twentieth century, featuring the following aspects (Ibid.: 58):

- Militaries glorified the offensive and adopted offensive military doctrines.
- Offensive actions were deemed to have the advantage in warfare, leading to the belief that wars would be short and decisive.
- Offensive strategies to national security problems were considered to be the most effective.

This approach was common to all of the superpowers. In Germany, "the military glorified the offense in strident terms, and inculcated German society with similar views" (Ibid.: 59). The common belief was that offense was superior to defense and that it was the most suitable strategy for ensuring victory in war. The notorious Schlieffen plan was entirely based on an offensive strategy with the aim of eliminating France from the game using a fast and powerful attack, and then moving the troops to the oriental front where the Russian troops would still be unprepared due to their long mobilization time.

In France things were no different. Quoting the words of the British military strategy historian Basil Liddel Hart, Stephen Van Evera writes that the French army became "obsessed with the virtues of the offensive" (Ibid.: 60). The French chief of staff, General Joffre, declared that the only true law of war lay in the launching of offensive attacks. The president of the French Republic, Clément Fallières, used to state that offensive strategies were those most suited to the spirit of French troops. Important members of the Parliament sustained similar ideas, and Marshal Foch exalted the power of offensive actions and of a strategy based on a decisive attack.

Although in a less exaggerated manner, other European States, such as England, Russia, and Italy, showed pro-offensive strategic cultures.[6] The Russian and British generals were all supporters of the superiority of offensive maneuvers compared to defensive ones. According to Van Evera, seeds of the cult of the offensive could be found even in a small country such as Belgium.[7]

Snyder (1984) focuses on the French, German, and Russian cases to reconstruct the causes of the development of the cult of the offensive on the brink of World War I. In the French case, the causes of the military's penchant for an offensive strategy are many. In the late nineteenth century in France there prevailed a moderately offensive culture featuring strong elements of flexibility so as to make it adaptable to various circumstances. In the decade prior to the outbreak of World War I, this strategic culture stiffened and was dogmatized, giving rise to a veritable cult of the offensive.

One factor that pushed in this direction was linked to internal political issues, more specifically to the need to defend the military institution and values in a period of crisis exacerbated by the eruption in 1894 of the Dreyfus affair. "In the years following the Dreyfus affair, the French military faced serious threats to its organizational autonomy and traditions, its doctrinal preference for the offensive, and its traditional formula for parrying a German invasion" (Ibid.: 70). The pressure put on by the political authorities led to the accentuation of professionalism and of offensive strategies. The implementation of a doctrine of offensive attack not only served operational purposes but also to lift the morale of the armed forces.

Another factor consisted in the ambiguity of the strategic situation. The lack of clarity with regard to Germany's intentions and its security policy led the military to interpret the clues they possessed through their predispositions. In the years prior to World War I, the German plans to increase the number of reservists had been kept secret. Lacking concrete proof of the nature of the threat, the French military pursued their planning according to their pro-offensive culture.

Finally, the strategic culture of the French was based on the underestimation of encirclement maneuvers (hence the lack of interest in the Belgian front) and on their preference for penetrating attacks.

In the case of the German General Staff, the cult of the offensive was determined by various elements. The Prussian officers were convinced that war was an inevitable characteristic of human relations and that it played a positive role by allowing the elimination of decadent nations and the assertion of young ones. They were influenced by the social Darwinism movement that in those years had crossed Europe like wildfire. In the period from 1890 to 1914, these ideas became most popular precisely in the field of international conflict. The idea of the struggle between single individuals for the selection of the fittest was replaced with that of the struggle between States. In the years leading up to the outbreak of the Great War, Social Darwinist theories were most widespread among the upper tiers of society and political class (Mayer 1981). Thus, if international relations are equivalent to the fight to survive, attacking first is widely justified.

Second, having achieved a high degree of prestige after their victory in the 1866 conflicts against the Austro-Hungarian Empire and in 1870–1871 against France, the German military aspired to consolidate their status by exalting the positive role of war. Their focus on the bellicose aspects of international relations allowed the military elite to reinforce their position in society. This could however be sustained only if war was fast and consisted of decisive attacks and maneuvers. Otherwise, if "wars are expected to be long, costly and indecisive, they are likely to be seen as aberrations that need to be stamped out—hardly a climate of opinion conducive to the prestige and health of military institutions" (Snyder 1984: 123).

Finally, Snyder argues that the German generals successors of Helmut von Moltke the Elder tended to have a more rigid and dogmatic outlook on offensive strategies. Moltke the Elder, the winner of the wars that had led to the construction of the German State, held a pragmatic position vis-à-vis strategy and, even though he preferred a war based on movement and on offensive actions, he was ready to change his strategy should the circumstances require it. Conversely, his heir Schlieffen was a dogmatic officer enraptured with the elegance of his plans and was less sensitive to the need of an elastic approach capable of responding to the ever-changing political-military conditions.

In the case of Russia, the factors that explain the cult of the offensive are three. The first derived from the rivalry within the armed forces between those who wanted to give priority to the Austrian front and those who preferred to concentrate troops on the German front. General Danilov, the major military planner of the Russian armed forces, was in favor of launching an offensive against Germany and of limiting the deployment of troops on the Austrian front. Alternately, General Alekseev, chief of staff of the military district of Warsaw and a very influential figure at court, championed an offensive against the Austro-Hungarian Empire. The impossibility of reaching an agreement between the two positions resulted in the disastrous decision to implement an offensive strategy on both fronts, consequently overexposing the Russian military forces.

The clashes between Danilov and Alekseev did not stem solely from their roles within the armed forces, but also from their different intellectual outlooks. Snyder argues that Danilov was a pessimist that did not believe in Russia's capability to face Germany alone. This belief had led him, in 1910, to draft a strongly defensive plan. A few years later, with France as an ally, Danilov's main concern was that Paris might capitulate before a German attack, leaving Moscow alone to wage the war. This, alongside his rivalry with Alekseev, drove him to plan an offensive strategy against Germany. Alekseev, on the contrary, was more optimistic and was convinced that a quick strike against Vienna would lead her to surrender.

The second factor that boosted the cult of the offensive derived from the General Staff's tendency to neglect logistic problems in planning, thereby underplaying the risks attributed to offensive actions. By not taking into consideration in war games—for budget reasons—prosaic problems such as provisioning, logistics, or the transport of troops, it was much simpler to choose offensive actions as their true difficulties were underestimated.

Third, the General Staff tended to consider a lengthy conflict detrimental for Russia and therefore deemed rapid aggressive actions essential. In short, what was necessary was also considered practicable. Since Russia could win only when the war was short and decisive, they tended to think that Russia was actually capable of conducting rapid attacks and of striking the enemy with a devastating blow.

Another two social scientists who have contributed in opening the path to the study of strategic cultures are Ken Booth and Colin Gray.

Booth has concentrated on the relationship between ethnocentrism and strategy. He defines the concept of strategic culture as including a nation's tradition, values, socially shared attitudes, and patterns of behavior with respect to the use of force (Booth 1990: 121). These elements have a cultural dimension in that they tend to resist the changes that can occur within the context of military technology and of the characteristics of the international system. The elements that compose a strategic culture can be referred to the entire nation, to part of the political elite, to the military, or to public opinion.

The study of strategic cultures is important for six reasons (Ibid.: 125–27). First of all, it allows to shed light on the relationship between ethnocentrism and military strategy. Booth attributes three meanings to the concept of ethnocentrism (Booth 1979: 14–15):

- A feeling of centrality and superiority of one's own group over another group.
- A technical term to describe a faulty methodology in social sciences, by which one's own frame of reference is projected onto others.
- A synonym for being "culture-bound," that is, an actor is unable to see international events through the eyes of an individual belonging to another culture.

Ethnocentrism generates a sort of "fog of culture" that leads to the misinterpretation of how to wage a war.

Second, the knowledge of strategic cultures improves the comprehension of the enemy and increases the chances of victory. This refers to the reasons for the cultural studies on the period relating to World War II.

Third, the concept of strategic culture increases sensitivity to the historical dimension of the international behavior of States.

Fourth, it allows to link together the domestic aspect of the decision-making process and the external behavior of the nations. "It reminds us that decision-making structure, military establishments and policy making processes all operate in peculiar political cultures" (Booth 1990: 126).

As a fifth reason, strategic culture helps understand behaviors that may appear totally irrational to observers from different cultures.

Finally, the study of strategic cultures allows to better evaluate the weight and meaning of the threats posed by other nations.

Colin Gray highlights the importance of studying the strategic culture of a country in order to avoid making mistakes in the attribution and interpretation of the enemy's actions and motivations. As he writes in an article in 1981 for *International Security* dedicated to the American military style: "In the late 1970s, American defense analysts 'discovered' something they had really known all along—that the Soviet Union did not appear to share many of the beliefs and practices that are central to the American idea of international order" (Gray 1981: 21). In the article, Gray continues by stating that:

- There is an American strategic culture and therefore an American national style in tackling military matters.
- The American strategic culture provides the milieu within which security issues are debated and defense policy are decided.
- An understanding of American strategic culture can help explain why American policy-makers have made the decisions they have.

Gray links the concept of strategic culture to that of political culture. Both concepts refer to the presence of a national style in making decisions. The strategic culture of a nation is affected by its geopolitical position, by its history, by economic characteristics, and by other factors peculiar to the specific national reality. Consequently, each nation learns (correctly or incorrectly) from its past events a set of lessons that give rise to a distinct way of conducting warfare (Gray 1984).

The history and geopolitical position of the United States have for a long time been characterized by insularity and the absence of serious threats to national security.[8] The consequence of these features was that policy-makers were not familiar with military problems in general and with strategic problems in particular. They had a scarce sense of history and were poorly acquainted with security problems. As Gray suggests, the American educational system tended mostly to favor the creation of experts in domestic problems. The result of the prevalence of these cultural models was that in the period under study (1960–1981) the American national style in the field of security featured the following traits (Gray 1981: 24):

- A leadership that was "managerial" rather than "strategic." This trend had its most extreme consequences in the administrative revolution introduced by the secretary of defense Robert McNamara in the early 1960s. He arrived at the Pentagon firmly convinced of the need to curb the weight of the military and their judgement in the decision-making process. McNamara held office as secretary of defense from 1961 to 1968. In these years, he worked with energy in reorganizing the department, and introduced planning criteria derived from the economic sector.
- The inability of American policy-makers to effectively come to grips with the prospect of war in the nuclear era. In the period of mutually assured destruction, the problem no longer consisted in how to best prepare to win the conflict with the enemy, bur rather in how to avoid the outbreak of such a conflict.[9] This meant that the loss of strategic superiority was not registered as a negative event but, rather, as a way of stabilizing Russian-American bilateral relations.

- The pursuance of an arms control process that, Gray states, was detrimental to the American interests.
- A mistaken interpretation of the Soviet rearmament process.
- Lack of comprehension of the Soviet Union's cultural diversity and of the consequent improbability that the USSR would behave according to American parameters.

In the period following the end of the Cold War, the widespread interest in cultural studies—the third wave—was caused, according to Desch (1998: 148–49), by the dissatisfaction in the neorealist explanations and their lack of interest in the internal characteristics of the States, and by the more general resurgence of interest in the role of ideational variables in explaining international relations, brought on by constructivism. A clear example of this fact is the work by Katzenstein and his coauthors (Katzenstein 1996a).[10] The following pages analyze three interesting cases that clearly illustrate the importance of this new wave. The first is the work by Elizabeth Kier on the development of military doctrine in France in the wake of the Versailles Treaty. The second is the work by Thomas Berger on the influence of cultural factors on the security policy of Germany and Japan in the post–World War II period. And finally, the work by Iain Johnston on the Chinese strategic culture that, thanks to its methodological accuracy, offers one of the best examples of cultural analysis of the military behavior of States and of the development of practices based on *realpolitik*.

Elizabeth Kier studied the effects of military organizational culture on the defense policy of France in between the two world wars.[11] In her research she focuses primarily on how the different subcultures of the Armed Forces and of the civilian leaders, as well as the interaction between these subcultures and the internal political dynamics, favored a shift from the preference for an offensive strategy, that dominated until World War I, to a strongly defensive one in the subsequent period.

Kier argues that the reason why the French military in the post–World War I period preferred a defensive doctrine must be sought in the domestic political debate regarding the role of the armed forces in society and in the way in which the military's organizational culture shaped the response to these events. Starting in the second half of the nineteenth century, France had seen the development of an intense debate between the right-wing and left-wing political forces over the function and organization of the armed forces. The right called for a professional army that, when needed, could be deployed to preserve law and order. The left, on the other hand, preferred an army based on conscripts, fearing that a professional army could easily become a tool for domestic repression in the hands of a reactionary government. This debate touched upon the problem of the length of conscription. The left argued that it should be as short as possible so as to prevent the development of an esprit de corps and prevent the soldiers' excessive dependence on their officers. Soldiers were supposed to be simple citizen-soldiers. Contrarily, the right favored long-term training because, it believed, this was the only way to make sure that in a domestic crisis the soldiers would be toughened and disciplined enough to implement repressive policies.

At the end of the 1920s, the French center-left wing parties promulgated a law reducing the length of conscription to one year, thus forcing the army to reform the military doctrine. Kier argues that the choice of a defensive strategy was absolutely not predetermined by structural factors. It was the type of organizational culture of the French army that drove the military services to adopt this type of solution. This would seem to prove the difficulties in the explanations of the neorealists who normally consider political-military choices as a response to some external threat/opportunity. In this case, the choice of the French policy-makers to reduce the length of conscription responded to domestic problems and had no relation to the threats coming from Germany.

> [. . .] French policymakers responded to domestic, not international factors when deciding on the organization structure of the army. The reduction in the term of conscription to one year responded to the left's fear of domestic threats, not to German capabilities or alliance diplomacy. The army reacted to this decision within the constraints of its organizational culture. Instead of choosing an offensive doctrine [. . .] the French army adopted a defensive doctrine (Kier 1995: 72).

The response of the French military to the shorter term of service was by no means a foregone conclusion and, according to Kier — who mentions the German case — another army with a different organizational culture could have reacted in a totally opposite manner to the decisions of the politicians. In the 1920s there were no objective conditions that would inevitably force the switch to a defensive doctrine. The French army did not lack the financial means necessary to plan for mobile warfare. In terms of equipment, there were no structural impediments to prevent the development of the technologies necessary to conduct preventive actions and attacks in depth. At a more doctrinal level, there were many ardent supporters of offensive actions based on mechanized and armored divisions, such as General De Gaulle. French civilian leaders neither supported a defensive option nor even thought of asking such a thing of the military. Not even the construction of the Maginot Line excluded offensive possibilities, since the network of fortifications initially was conceived to buttress offensive operations. "The French army had the money, ideas and freedom to adopt an offensive doctrine, but instead it chose a defensive doctrine. Its organizational culture would not allow otherwise" (Ibid.: 74).

So, what were the characteristics of the French army's organizational culture that drove them to adopt this strategy? The French military were convinced that a one-year term of conscription cold not produce soldiers capable of engaging in offensive actions. Short-term conscripts would not be able to handle the technology for implementing mobile warfare, nor they had the type of spirit or discipline necessary for offensive actions. This point of view was shared by many top ranks of the French army, who all agreed that an army of short-term conscripts was good only for defending the borders behind fortified positions.

In those same years in which the French officers stated the impossibility of using conscripts to conduct modern warfare consisting of encircling maneuvers and attacks in depth, the German officers—with their different organizational culture—stated exactly the opposite, namely that "reserve troops will be employed in the same way as active troops" (quoted in Ibid.: 75).

By adopting a definition of culture taken from the sociologist Ann Swidler, Kier states that a culture firstly defines the means for action rather than the goals pursued.[12] The military cultures shaped the preferences of the armed forces with regard to a given type of weapon, a given type of strategy, a given type of organization. Faced with the need to accept an army of short-term conscripts, the French military had no choice but to take the path indicated by their organizational culture as the correct one.[13]

Thomas Berger analyzes the emergence of a pacifist political-military culture in Germany[14] and Japan in the post–World War II period and its impact on these two States' security policies. Unlike Kier, who focuses on the subcultures of the military, Berger takes into consideration the strategic culture of the entire nation. This implies greater methodological complications (Berger 1996: 328):

> The study of the political-military culture of an entire nation requires a detailed, multilayered research strategy, involving three central empirical tasks. First, it is necessary to investigate the original set of historical experiences that define how a given society views the military, national security, and the use of force, paying careful attention to the interpretation of these events among different groups in the society. Second, one needs to examine the political process through which actual security policy was made and how particular decisions were subsequently legitimated. In this context it is important to define the essential features of both the political-military culture and the security policy associated with it at a *particular point in time*. Third, it is necessary to examine the evolution of both the political-military culture and defense policies over time, monitoring how they evolved in response to historical events.

Berger analyzes the way in which the political-military cultures of the two powers defeated in WWII have affected their national identity, the level of military expenditure, the role of the Armed Forces in society, and the inclination for the use of force.[15] He defines political-military culture as "a subset of the larger political culture that influences how members of a given society view national security, the military as an institution, and the use of force in international relations" (Ibid.: 325–26).

The end of the 1940s and the early 1950s are considered crucial in explaining the development of Germany's and Japan's political-military cultures.[16] It is in those years that the intellectual bases for the definition of the security problems of the two States were developed. The debate was not limited to technical issues—such as which was the best way to organize defense—but expanded to more in-depth issues about how the two nations defined their political identity, their domestic interests and the type of economic and political systems to adopt.

The post–World War II history of the two nations shows a clear break from the immediate past that featured ardent militarism. In both cases, the armed forces had played an essential role in constructing the nation, enjoyed a very high status and were highly influential within society.[17] The disastrous outcome of the war threw discredit on the more extremist components of the two societies and on the military leaders, considered to be the driving forces behind the policies that led to Japan's occupation by the United States, and Germany's split into two parts. As foretold by Vasquez's model,[18] this resulted in the emergence of a stable leadership that refused to use force as a tool for handling international relations. The populations rejected the more extreme forms that had been the feature of their national policies in between the two world wars.

According to Berger, serious military defeat alone cannot explain the repudiation of the previous aggressive and nationalist political-military cultures. The American occupation forces and the emergence of new leaderships played an essential role, too. The United States applied a policy of demilitarization of the two societies, not only by dismantling their military-industrial complex but also by operating at a psychological and cultural level to delete militarist values. Among other things, for the first time in history, the German and Japanese leaders who had most represented the values of the most aggressive militarism were put on trial and in many cases sentenced to death. This external action was flanked by that of the new ruling classes that included persons who were deeply suspicious of the prewar militarist culture. Both the left-wing and the right-wing forces, albeit to different extents, had a strategic culture that featured pacifist elements. In the years following the beginning of the Cold War, this affected the rearmament programs supported by the United States to counter the Soviets.

The effects of the antimilitarist culture on the security policies of Germany and Japan were many. Japan developed a national identity in which it proclaimed itself as a trading State mainly interested in economic development and hostile to military rearmament and to the search for national power. As regards international relations, the focus of Tokyo's foreign policy was the alliance with Washington. This was a relationship of dependency in which Japan, albeit playing the role of faithful ally, had a rather passive attitude in order to avoid becoming too involved in America's international adventures. This attitude resulted in a low percentage of the GDP allocated to military expenditure, the refusal of nuclear weapons, and a nonaggressive configuration of the armed forces structured basically for domestic defense.[19] As regards civil-military relations, the civilian leaders, unlike in the previous period, enjoyed supremacy over the military establishment.

The consequences for West Germany were similar. Bonn boosted the process of European integration, considering it as the most suitable institutional framework for ensuring the country's rebirth and avoid nationalistic temptations. Like Japan, Germany joined the Atlantic Alliance but with a more active approach, given its position of strategic vulnerability. In terms of the structure of military forces, it renounced the development of nuclear weapons and established that the military instrument could be used only for defense reasons under the NATO umbrella. As for the civil-military relations, the Armed Forces were democratized and put under close political control. Mandatory conscription was enforced.

Despite the changes that have occurred in the post–Cold War international system, and that have triggered heated debate over the political-military culture of the two States, "the general direction of the shifts in German and Japanese attitudes and behaviors indicates a consolidation rather than an abandonment of the antimilitarism approaches to national security of the 1950s" (Ibid.: 355–56).

Johnston studied the strategic culture of China and its impact on Beijing's international behavior (1995b; 1996). He defines strategic culture as a set of beliefs about war and the role of the military force from which a set of hierarchically ordered operational preferences are derived. Johnston argues that the idea that Chinese strategic culture is monolithic and dominated by the Confucian model is incorrect. Next to the Confucian-Mencian culture there exists a second cultural tradition that he defines as *parabellum*. In the Confucian-Mencian model, war is considered to be an aberration and not a normal form of conduct in international relations. Adversaries are not seen as implacable enemies placing a mortal threat, but as actors with whom it is possible to have cooperative relations and accomplish forms of pacific coexistence through policies of enculturation and co-optation. It follows that the use of force in managing international relations must be limited to the utmost degree. This leads to the preference for strategies of compromise over offensive actions, with defensive strategies taking a middle position.

According to Johnston, at operational (concrete action) level, the *parabellum* model, that essentially is rooted in realism, was more important that the first. This model considers war a normal aspect of interstate relations, and the adversary as a threat to be eliminated with force; consequently, the best policy is to attack first. The reason why the Confucian model seems to have held sway lies in the fact that often political actions based on the *parabellum* model were disguised by the moralistic language and rhetoric pertaining to the other model.

To support his theory, Johnston analyzes the *Seven Military Classics* of Ancient China, using them to reconstruct the international politics concept and the strategic prescriptions of Chinese culture. The *Seven Military Classics* are the following:

1. *The Art of War* by Sun Zi, most probably written in about 500 B.C.
2. *The Art of War* by Wu Qi, slightly more recent, written by the student of a disciple of Confucius.
3. *The Methods* by Sima Rangju, a military official of the State of Qi, dated around the third century B.C.
4. *The Art of War* by Wei Liao, the dating of which is uncertain although most probably it has been written in the fourth century B.C.
5. *The Six Secret Strategic Teachings* by Jiang Tai Gong, dating back to the final period of the Warring States (end of the third century B.C.).
6. *The Three Strategies* by Huang Shi Gong, dated more or less like the previous text.
7. *Questions and Replies between Tang Tai Zhong and Li Wei Gong*. A more recent book, dating back to the tenth century.

By using content analysis, Johnston reconstructs the concept that dominated in imperial China with regard to the role of war, the nature of the enemies, State security and the best way to achieve it.

> War is considered a relatively constant characteristic of the human condition. Whether one resorts to war or not depends on the adversary. It is the enemy's disposition that determines whether one faces a security threat. This disposition to war is, by definition, unrighteous, since the moral order requires one not to threaten the security of another. One's own resort to force, therefore, is not only legitimate and necessary, it is not bounded by any a priori moral limits, since the enemy is beyond the pale. The utter defeat of the enemy requires the application of superior force. An analysis of the cause-effect statements in the military classics suggests that violence is highly efficacious and that nonviolent strategies in general do not lead directly to the submission of the enemy, but that they are at most a prelude to the application of overwhelming military power (Johnston 1995b: 106).

This vision translates into a positive evaluation of offensive policies. In all of the studies, excepting *The Three Strategies* by Huang Shi Gong, that provides strategic preferences consistent with the Confucian model (compromise policies ranked first, defense second, and offensive actions third), accommodation strategies are ranked third among the options preferred for ensuring State security. As regards the offensive actions and defensive policies, no clear-cut preference emerges for either one, although there appears to be a certain inclination for the offensive ones (Ibid.: 148).

The analysis of the security policy of the Ming period (1368–1644) confirms the strength of the *parabellum* model compared to the Confucian one. Ming policy-makers considered war a natural and inescapable aspect of international relations. In particular, they considered as an unchangeable historical condition the conflict with the Mongols who were considered aggressive and desirous of overtaking China's riches. The inevitable conflict with the Mongol populations could be overcome only through a preponderant display of military force.

> By accepting the three basic assumptions of the *parabellum* paradigm, Ming's strategic choices were affected by the real or imagined consequences of appearing weak in the face of the insatiable Mongols [. . .] At a minimum, the fear that weakness would undermine the credibility of future political-military actions meant that accommodationist strategies were least preferred to violent ones, whether defensive or offensive. At a maximum, Ming *parabellum* thought dictated that offensive strategies were, in principle, the most preferred, since anything less was a signal of weakness that would only encourage Mongol aggressiveness (Ibid.: 215).

Later on, Johnston (1996) applied his model to the study of the strategic culture of contemporary China, showing how Marxism-Leninism and its positive attitude towards the use of force increased the importance of the *parabellum* model in contemporary China's strategic culture. He applied the same technique used for the *Seven Military Classics* to some of Mao Zedong's most renowned works on strategy and warfare:

- *Problems of Strategy in China's Revolutionary War*, written in 1936. This essay summarizes the military teachings deriving from civil war. It starts with a general analysis of the laws of war, then goes on to specify the laws of revolutionary war and, finally, at an even more detailed level, the laws of revolutionary war in China.
- *On the New Stage*, written in 1938. This is an article on the creation of an anti-Japanese united front. It puts in second place the problem of the conflict with Chiang Kai-shek in view of a joint effort to defeat the common enemy.
- *The Present Situation and Our Tasks*, written in 1947. This text outlines the strategies for the final overthrow of the Guomindang nationalists and the establishment of a new State.
- *Mao's Moscow Conference Speech*, given in 1957. This speech was not a proper military strategy essay but rather a broader discussion on statecraft and the role of power in social relations.

From Johnston's close examination of these works one infers Mao's ideas with regard to political conflict and the role of violence. According to Mao, war is a natural component of social relations. One can discern a sort of similarity between the Confucian image of the enemy and that of Marxism-Leninism. While in the first model it is right to fight a nation that conducts itself immorally, in the same way, according to Marxist-Leninist thought, it is right to fight a class enemy oppressing another class or another nation. As for the role of violence, it is considered an effective tool, as witnessed by Mao's famous statement about power growing out of a gun barrel. The strategic preferences appear congruent with the *parabellum* model. Mao gave priority to the active defense strategy that, beyond its name, included the option of conducting offensive actions and of striking the enemy first, exploiting the element of surprise. The analysis of China's actual behavior in the military sector from 1949 to the present time seems to confirm the weight of the *parabellum* model and the importance of military force in the strategic culture of Chinese policymakers.[20]

METHODOLOGICAL DIFFERENCES IN THE VARIOUS SCHOLAR GENERATIONS

Johnston distinguishes between three generations of strategic culture studies,[21] that do not coincide exactly with the three historical waves listed by Desch. Johnston's division aims at distinguishing the various studies by their methodology.

The first generation of work on strategic culture includes studies conducted between the end of the 1970s and the early 1980s on the behavior of the United States and USSR in the field of nuclear strategy. Johnston places authors such as Snyder, Booth, and Gray, who are included in Desch's second wave, into this generation. He argues that although they had the great merit of pioneering cultural research in the strategic studies sector, that had been dominated until then by formal models of economic origin, they had many methodological shortcomings. The first regards the definition itself of the concept of strategic culture. "Technology, geography, organizational culture and traditions, historical strategic practices, political culture, national character, political psychology, ideology, and even international system structure were all considered relevant inputs into this amorphous strategic culture" (Johnston 1995a: 37). The overabundance of factors makes it almost impossible to identify a specific contribution of the strategic culture concept. It becomes a residual variable next to all other independent variables normally used by researchers of security issues.[22]

A second shortcoming, according to Johnston, consists in the fact that the first generation of strategic studies included observed behavioral models in the definition of culture. This made it difficult to distinguish ideational factors from their actual effect.[23] This manner of viewing the problem produced a sort of determinism that established a univocal correspondence between a given strategic culture and a given type of behavior.

Gray (1999) strikes back heavily on this point, claiming the validity of his concept of culture. He criticizes Johnston's insistence on separating belief systems from the actual behaviors in which they are expressed, in order to develop empirically verifiable theories. Gray argues that strategic culture is nothing but the sedimented way in which people's reactions to given military problems are expressed. The "cultural" feature does not derive so much from the fact that it refers to ideational factors but rather from the element of temporal stability that these behaviors acquire, such as to allow the definition of a national strategic style.[24] The strategic culture is the context within which political-military choices are made. Gray denies any validity of Johnston's positivist method. "The problem is that we cannot understand strategic behavior by that method, be it ever so rigorous. Strategic culture is not only 'out there,' it is also within us; we, our institutions, and our behavior are the context [. . .] strategic culture offers context, not reliable causality" (Ibid.: 53, 62).

Having stated these points, Gray indicates the contributions offered by the analysis of strategic cultures:

- Strategic behavior is always determined by culture, as the product of the choices of people who are socialized within a given culture.
- This cultural element does not disappear even under severe structural pressure.
- Strategic culture is a guide to action, not in the sense that it is an independent variable, as Johnston suggests, but in the sense that people always carry this baggage with them.
- Normally, a nation has a dominant strategic culture.
- Strategic cultures can generate dysfunctional behaviors.
- Strategic cultures can be referred to various levels of analysis—the nation as a whole, grand strategy, single armed forces,[25] different generations of policy-makers, etc.

In his reply to Gray, Johnston (1999) once again defines what he considers the intrinsic shortcomings of the first generation: determinism, incapability to separate the independent variable from the dependent one, considering societies as characterized by homogeneous strategic cultures, and so on. If the cultural variables are nothing but a part of the context in which strategic decisions are made, how is it possible to separate these variables from the other and understand their contribution to the explanation? The actual problem is that Gray is less interested in understanding the specific contribution of the cultural variables and more in producing an exhaustive explanation of the strategic behavior of a country.

To sum up, Johnston's criticism of the first generation of strategic culture studies consists in that they assign too much (or not enough) importance to cultural variables. In some studies, the cultural variable explains everything, thus establishing a precise and direct relationship between culture and strategic behavior. Conversely, in other works its role remains undetermined, since it is only one of the many elements of a context that affects strategic choices, making it absolutely impossible to establish its weight.

The second generation of literature on strategic culture, appearing in the mid-1980s, features an instrumental vision of ideational factors. The works belonging to this generation tend to consider the cultures as a simple rhetorical expedient for covering actions whose motivations can be found in totally different contexts. There would be a gap between the States' declaratory policies and their operational planning. While the former intend to convince public opinion about the validity of the decision taken, the latter follow military logic that cannot be stated in the open.[26]

Johnston replies to this approach by underlining the fact that, even in the event of a purely symbolical use of strategic culture, this wouldn't necessarily mean that it has no actual effect on the behavior of the policymakers. "Rhetorical entrapment" phenomena may occur, which means that people are influenced by the same arguments they created to legitimize their actions. "[. . .] elites, too, are socialized in the strategic culture they produce, and thus can be constrained by the symbolic myths which their predecessors created" (Johnston 1995a: 40).

The second generation of studies is incapable of producing generalizations as regards the military behavior of nations. On the one hand, since strategic culture is a simple rhetorical expedient, all States should follow the imperatives of the *realpolitik* and not show any significant differences. On the other, the considerations regarding rhetorical entrapment lead to the belief that the use of a strategic culture may limit the number of options available to a government, and push in different directions the States' military behavior.

The third generation of studies on strategic cultures—which emerged in the 1990s—tends to be more rigorous in its methodology and more specific in defining its dependent and independent variables. The studies conducted by Kier and by Berger, the research performed by Katzenstein, and Johnston's own analysis are some of this generation's most important examples. This generation features three main characteristics.

First, it avoids using the overly deterministic assertions typical of the first generation. This is because these researchers keep separate the cultural factors, intended as independent variables, from the behaviors observed, that constitute the dependent variable. The former will not necessarily produce clear effects on the latter.

Second, third generation studies are committed to verifying the different explicative power of the various approaches. Theories derived from various models are compared and, through the collection of empirical data, they are tested in order to see which are those that produce the most satisfactory explanations. A collective work edited by Glenn, Howlett, and Poore (2004) follows this path. By means of a cross-national comparison, they attempt to verify the explicative value of the cultural and the structural variables proposed by neorealism.

Third, all of these works share a similar concept of culture: "culture either presents decision-makers with a limited range of options or it acts as a lens that alters the appearance and efficacy of different choices" (Johnston 1995a: 42).

THE EMPIRICAL STUDY OF STRATEGIC CULTURES AND THE ITALIAN CASE

Starting from the assessment of the three different generations of studies, Johnston proposes a research design that in a rigorous and empirically verifiable manner redefines the strategic cultures and their impact on the international behavior of States. This implies a clear definition of the problem, the identification of an adequate research method and the construction of empirical indicators.[27]

In order to study Italy's strategic culture and its impact on foreign policy, I have used Johnston's definition, who—based on the work by Clifford Geertz (1977)—defines strategic culture as a system of symbols that expresses a society's prevailing ideas about (Johnston 1995a: 46–47):

1. The role of war in international relations (war can be considered a normal aspect of interstate relations or as a momentary aberration), the nature of the adversaries (they can be considered pacific or implacable enemies), the efficacy of the use of force (the military tool can be effective in achieving one's own goals or generates useless violence).
2. The ranking of the various strategic options (offensive actions, defensive actions, nonmilitary actions).

The advantage of this definition is that it is clear, exhaustive, and distinguishes the more closely symbolic factors (the first half of the definition regarding the belief systems) from operational factors (the second half of the definition regarding the strategic preferences of the policy-makers) that are more directly connected to behavior. Johnston indicates which are the cultural "objects" to analyze in order to reconstruct a strategic culture: theoretical writings, operational plans, debates, public declarations, national symbols, preferences for specific weapon systems, images conveyed to the public opinion, etc.[28]

The empirical study of strategic cultures implies various stages:

1. Identification of the main cultural elements: images of war, of the adversary and of the role of force held by the political and military elites, keeping in mind that different strategic subcultures may co-exist within the same country.[29]
2. Identification of the preferred strategic options and of the consistency, if any, between these and the beliefs on the use of force.
3. Analysis of the actual military behavior of a country in order to verify the congruency between the belief systems, the strategic preferences and the political decisions taken.

In the second part of this book I will attempt to apply this research scheme to Italy's strategic culture.

NOTES

1. In the pact of alliance between Germany and Italy, one reads: "The governments of Japan, Germany and Italy consider it as the condition precedent to any lasting peace that all nations of the world be given each its proper station." In the statement handed to the American government after Pearl Harbor, one reads: "It is the immutable policy of the Japanese Government [. . .] to enable each nation to find each its proper place in the world." Both documents are quoted in Benedict (2005: 44).
2. Alexander George (1969), in his article on the operational code of political leaders, highlights how an important component of operational codes regards the belief in the possibility of predicting social events.
3. This part regarding the deterrence policy partially draws from Foradori, Rosa, Scartezzini (2008: 274–78).
4. Kahn's Escalation Ladder consists of forty-four rungs, separated by six thresholds. The third threshold is the most important because it marks the passage from an armed conflict in which nuclear weapons are not used to one in which they start being used, even if only against limited military targets.
5. In nuclear strategy terminology, counterforce strategy is defined as the strategy aimed at attacking the enemy's military targets, while countervalue strategy is the strategy aimed at attacking civilian targets (cities and industrial centers).
6. The Italian case will be analyzed in depth in the next chapter.
7. As regards the diffusion of the cult of the offensive related to World War I, see also Michael Howard (1986: 510): "When war broke out in Europe in August 1914, every major belligerent power at once took the offensive. The Austro-Hungarian army invaded Poland. The Russians invaded East Prussia. The Germans invaded France through Belgium; and the French tried to recapture their lost provinces of Alsace and Lorraine [. . .] The attacks continued through 1915, when Italy attacked Austria."
8. As Stephen Krasner wrote (1978: 66): "America has never needed a strong State. The political, social and economic imperatives that have enhanced the role of the State in Japan and continental Europe have been much less compelling in the United States. First, with one minor exception (the War of 1812), the United States has never been confronted with foreign invasion."
9. Samuel Huntington (1961: 26) defines this transformation as a shift from a preparedness to a deterrence policy.
10. To this regard, see chapter 2.
11. The following is derived from Kier (1995; 1996).
12. Culture is "a 'tool-kit' of symbols, stories, rituals, and world-views, which people may use in varying configurations to solve different kinds of problems [. . .] it

focuses on 'strategies of actions,' persistent ways of ordering actions through time" (Swidler 1986: 273).

13. Kier's work is especially interesting with regard to the Italian case, since one of the various reasons indicated for the low-profile adopted by Italian foreign policy is also the fact that Italy's armed forces—for a long time based on insufficiently trained conscripts—were considered unsuitable for carrying out force projection missions or missions in crisis areas.

14. The reference is to West Germany.

15. Given the common historical experience—serious military defeat, passage from authoritarian regimes to democratic ones, implementation of Constitutions with strong pacifist elements—the study of the strategic cultures of Germany and Japan is especially significant for comprehending Italy's case, too.

16. The following is a summary from Berger (1996).

17. As regards the position of absolute dominancy of the military in Japanese society, see Benedict (2005).

18. See chapter 2.

19. To this regard, see Lind (2004).

20. Johnston writes about China's behavior in militarized interstate disputes (MID) (1998b: 17): "The data suggest, then, that in general China has been more dispute-prone than many other major powers (except the United States); it has also been more likely than most other major powers to resort to higher levels of force when in a militarized dispute, regardless of the type of dispute. While the first 15 years of its existence were more dispute-prone than the subsequent 25, there has been a fairly constant level of hostility and violence across Chinese MIDs up to the end of the 1980s. While average violence scores were quite consistent across all types of disputes, China tended to resort to the highest scale of military action ('clashes') in territorial disputes."

21. The following section draws mainly from Johnston (1995a). As for the characteristics of these three generations, see also Duffield (1999) and Poore (2004).

22. This is Desch's position when he argues that the cultural explanations of the strategic behavior of States can, at most, help to comprehend the delay with which the States adapt to international changes, or why sometimes they pursue deviant behaviors, or to explain behavior in environments in which it is not sufficiently clear which is the most efficient strategy (Desch 2005). In short, the studies on strategic cultures can support realist studies but cannot replace them.

23. "[. . .] cultural explanations are rendered tautological through the derivation of inferences about culture from behavior" (Duffield 1999: 773).

24. Even Snyder (1990: 6) seems to agree on this point when he writes that "[a]part from bogus cultural explanations, which simply point to a cross-national difference and label it cultural, there are two kinds of explanation in which the cultural component does play a real role. The first, of which the author is dubious, is the explanation of strategic doctrines in terms of national or elite political culture. The second, which he considers more fruitful, shows how distinctive strategic patterns take on a kind of cultural persistence through the effects of socialization and institutionalization and through their role in social legitimation."

25. This is the position held by Yitzhak Klein (1991) who defines strategic cultures as: "the set of attitudes and beliefs held by a military establishment concerning the political objectives of war and the most effective strategy and operational method of achieving them."

26. The work Johnston refers to as exemplifying this approach is that by Bradley Klein (1988).

27. The same direction has been taken by the research conducted by Jeffrey Lantis (2009).

28. "Strategic culture refers to collectively held preferences, and analysis focuses on collectively produced and shared cultural artifacts" (Johnston 1995a: 48 note 31).

29. As regards the reasons for concentrating on political and administrative elites, see Duffield (1999: 793–94): "First, elite political culture is typically easier to describe and measure comprehensively [. . .] Second, political culture as revealed in the attitudes of elites is likely to be more elaborate and detailed [. . .] Third, as suggested by the definition of political elites, elite attitudes are likely to have a much more immediate bearing on State behavior."

II

Italy's Strategic Culture and Foreign Policy

FOUR

Italy's Strategic Culture

In part two, I analyze the Italian strategic culture and its impact on foreign policy. The first paragraphs of chapter 4 contains an overview of the images of war and of adversaries, an assessment of the military instrument and the strategic preferences of the political and military elites in the Liberal (1861–1921) and Fascist (1922–1943/45)[1] periods. The second paragraph analyzes the historical and political causes leading to the formation of the current strategic culture in the aftermath of military defeat (1946–2008), and its key features.

THE CHARACTERISTICS OF ITALIAN STRATEGIC CULTURE IN THE LIBERAL AND FASCIST PERIODS

Before discussing how strategic culture developed in Italy after World War II, I analyze how warfare and the use of force was conceived by the Italian elites during the Liberal and Fascist periods. This will improve our understanding of the profound and dramatic changes after the end of World War II.

On the eve of World War I, Italy shared the "cult of the offensive" with the other European powers. Maneuver warfare, preventive strikes, taking the war into enemy territory were the mainstays of strategic planning. When Italy was still considering entering the war alongside Germany and Austria-Hungary, the General Staff was prepared to send an army corps to the Rhine to help implement the Schlieffen Plan, which was based on a lightning two-pronged offensive against France, to be completed before Russia entered the war.[2] However, after the reversal of alliances, Italian General Luigi Cadorna hatched plans providing for a rapid advance into the heart of the Austro-Hungarian Empire to deal the enemy a severe blow and crush it as swiftly as possible.[3]

In February 1915, with all the risks inherent in an offensive strategy now evident, and the European armies bogged down in a bloody trench warfare, the Italian General Staff sent out a circular on frontal assault and the advantages of the offensive.[4] It was as if the army officers' mentality was impermeable to the news arriving from the battlefield. The document, sent with great urgency to all those responsible for the armed forces, earnestly recommended to abide by the new instructions, which replaced or integrated the indications contained in a previous circular sent out shortly after the outbreak of hostilities, in August 1914. Its significance is enhanced by the fact that, being a tactical document, it focused on operational matters and did not contain reflections on general nature of the war. As far as the use of rearguard troops was concerned, which had to be deployed in maneuver attacks, the documents stated that "although they enter the stage later on, they are actors in the same drama, and their concerted efforts must have the same effect as the overwhelming final blow delivered in battle by Napoleon's armies" (Chiefs of Staff Command 1915: 24). The reference to the Napoleonic wars is a clear indication that the mindset of the officers who drafted the circular was still firmly rooted in offensive maneuver warfare.

Apparently, the Italian General Staff, just like their other European counterparts, had not been particularly impressed by the modernization of firearms and their impact on the balance between offense and defense. The only clue we have of any concern in this respect was the recommendation not to attack—as in the past—by concentrating large numbers of soldiers in one point, so as not to expose them to enormous risk. The assaults had to be carried out "using successive waves of men, widely spread out." In the conclusion to the first section it was explicitly stated (Ibid.: 32, 33, original italics):

> We may, therefore, infer that modern weapons have produced the following advantages for the offensive (besides those of an essentially moral order, which have always ensured its prevalence over the defensive):
>
> 1. *The possibility for the attacking artillery to use covered positions for more time and with greater advantage, compared to the defense, and to overpower it when it is obliged to expose itself as a result of the advance* (and consequent approach) *of the infantry.*
>   *A more effective convergence of the artillery fire and of the attacking infantry on the objectives to be conquered* [. . .]
>
> Therefore, there are more favorable conditions today for the offensive to be successful than in the past.

This approach tended to downscale the importance of trench warfare. Passive defense was considered ineffective, and the outcome of the conflict depended on a robust offensive action. Therefore, "when one of the two sides in conflict really feels stronger than its opponent it will launch an offensive, which is the only way of achieving a decisive outcome: it will definitely be the maneuver that decides the course of the war" (Ibid.: 34).

The fact that the confidence of the military planners was not in the least shaken can be explained only by their dogmatic approach to strategic issues. Among the military elite, the cult of the offensive descended directly from the prevailing convictions, at the time, regarding the role of war in international relations, the image of the adversaries, and the use of the military instrument for achieving national objectives.

On the eve of the Great War, the European ruling elites were still dominated by a system of beliefs rooted in the preindustrial world. Positions of power were held by members of the old nobility (Mayer 1981). The top government officials were aristocrats, who embodied values among which militarism had pride of place. The king decided the foreign policy together with his court. For these men, in most cases, "to act [meant] to undertake military ventures" (Schumpeter 1972: 61).

The Italian ruling class was no exception. The ideas underlying the doctrine of the *machtstaat*, which stressed the expansionist nature of the State, the conflictual nature of international politics and the central role of military power, and the Social Darwinist theories, which emphasized how subjugation was a key component in social relations, were widespread among policy-makers. The positive role assigned to war by the liberal politicians clearly emerges in the words of Francesco Crispi, and other Italian political men, as mentioned by Fortunato Minniti (Minniti 2006: 37-38): "A nation of 31 million inhabitants that disappears, that hides, that counts for nothing in the world, is just a geographical figure, not a power" and is therefore destined to succumb, even as a unitary State. We must not, Crispi continues, "close our eyes for fear of the light." On the contrary, we must open them wide and contemplate recourse to war.

In Crispi's vision, war played an essential role in solving the political contrasts between the great powers. He gave an optimistic assessment of the effectiveness of the military instrument for accomplishing his objectives: strengthening the State, achieving the status of great power, and colonial expansion (Ibid.: 50–51).[5]

The belief systems of Italian policy-makers of the time are well schematized in Chabod's portraits of several key politicians who drafted the foreign policy of the Liberal period: Emilio Visconti Venosta, Costantino Nigra, Count de Launay, Count di Robilant, Giovanni Lanza, Marco Minghetti, Vittorio Emanuele II.[6]

Marquis Emilio Visconti Venosta served a number of times as minister of foreign affairs. He began his diplomatic career in 1863 and last held office from 1899 to 1901. According to Chabod, he was a very pragmatic man, not prone to recklessness. He did not try to bend events to his will, nor wanted to let himself be dragged down by them, preferring to go along with them until the right time came to put his stamp on the circumstances. His attitude towards the use of force was rather flexible. For example, he disapproved of the use of military force to take Rome, but once the city had been taken he supported the operation wholeheartedly. Visconti Venosta had a very complex personality, combining elements of *realpolitik* and Liberal tendencies that stressed the moral dimension of international relations. He was a Machiavellian, but at the same time he considered it wrong to justify the use of certain means and to separate public from private ethics. He was a classic diplomat, in the mold of Metternich and Kaunitz. He believed that the principle of the balance of power was of fundamental importance for the future of Europe, but he was also in favor of recognizing the national aspiration of peoples and did not view foreign policy as being entirely separate from domestic politics. Although he gave great importance to international trade, and to the possibility of founding the world order on peaceful relations, he nevertheless thought that this type "of approach [required] peaceful and reasonable peoples" (Chabod 1965: 669), a condition that was far from being achieved at the end of the nineteenth century.

Costantino Nigra—as Italian ambassador to Paris (1860), Saint Petersburg (1876), London (1882), and Vienna (1885)—played a key role in shaping Italy's foreign policy at the end of the nineteenth century. He belonged to the Romantic period, and his mindset and diplomatic style were very similar to those of Visconti Venosta, from which he differed for a more disenchanted and pessimistic view of politics. Although, for his cynicism and impersonality, he has been compared to Talleyrand, unlike this latter he was strongly loyal and alien to any form of opportunism. He was a convinced supporter of international peace and of the need to moderate national feelings, in order not to upset the delicate European balances.

Count Edoardo de Launay, who served as an ambassador in important European capitals, was another key figure in the creation of the foreign policy of the Liberal period. He spent decisive years at the Italian Embassy in Berlin, from where he participated in the negotiations leading to the cornerstone of Italian international politics at the time, the Triple Alliance Treaty of 1882, and its renewal of 1887. He was the doyen of Italian diplomacy and represented the old realist school, which placed national interest before anything else. Foreign policy, he maintained, was a difficult art that could not be left in the amateurish hands of the politicians; it needed to be conducted with an appropriate degree of discretion and secrecy. His ideas and values were the exact opposite of those of Visconti Venosta. While the latter was a Liberal, Count de Launay was a conservative, an admirer of Chancellor Bismarck. The former was Francophile, the latter pro-German, convinced as he was that Italy's destiny as a great power could only be accomplished through a war against France.

The Count of Robilant was related, through descent and marriage, to the top European aristocratic families. Before entering diplomacy, he had had an intense military career. He had fought in the Wars of Independence and, from 1867 to 1871, had served as Commander of the War School. He was then Ambassador in Vienna and Ministry of Foreign Affairs. Unlike de Launay, he was not favorable to traditional secret diplomacy, which he considered outdated. A moderate conservative, he was allergic to parliamentary politics and to political party dynamics. As a result of this attitude, he believed in the primacy of foreign policy over domestic politics and, therefore, in the need to put aside domestic political and ideological contrasts in order to pursue the national interest.

Alongside these figures, there are the two presidents of the Council of Ministers, Giovanni Lanza and Marco Minghetti, both deeply attached to Visconti Venosta and his policy. Minghetti, however, more flexible than Visconti Venosta, changed his stance, abandoning the alliance with France and siding with Germany (he had a great admiration for Germany's chancellor).

The last key player in Liberal Italy's foreign policy was the king, Vittorio Emanuele II, who, like all sovereigns of the time, including constitutional monarchs, considered foreign and military policy a preserve of the crown. As far as international relations were concerned, the king's education dated back to the Napoleonic era, when diplomacy was conducted mostly through direct personal and secret contacts. Although less active after 1870, Vittorio Emanuele continued to play an important role in the formulation of the country's foreign policy. As Chabod puts it (Ibid.: 709):

> Foreign and military affairs continued to be the two fields of national life in which he showed a lively interest, consistently with the centuries-long tradition of his and other reigning houses: a tradition rooted in the Age of Absolutism, when [. . .] the life of the State could be summed up in either its diplomatic activities, for the purpose of preventing or promoting war, or its military actions, the end of which was to support the throne and perhaps gain territorial acquisitions in the process. Although d'Azeglio's myth had consecrated him as the Gentleman King, Vittorio Emanuele was instinctively a soldier and, wishfully at least, a maker of diplomatic plots.

This group of policy-makers, who belonged to the aristocracy and the upper classes by way of their culture and tradition, despite their Liberal vision of foreign policy (Vigezzi 1991), found it natural to think in terms of balance of power, security and national interest and, if the circumstances required, to resort to the use of military power.

> The political decisions regarding Italy's intervention in World War I, and Italian diplomacy during the conflict, were taken by politicians and senior officials such as Avarna, Bollati, Imperiali, San Giuliano, Tittoni, Salandra, and Sonnino, who were loyal to the foreign policy

tenets established and consolidated since the time of the Triple Alliance. They were inspired by the traditional values of Italian foreign policy, grounded on an elite vision of diplomacy, and with classic political and strategic objectives (Monzali 2005: 29).

Italy's historic enemy was Austria-Hungary. The expression used to describe relations between the two countries was *Erbfeindschaft*: perennial enmity. Three wars had been waged against Austria: the First War of Independence, in 1848, was fought by a coalition of Italian States led by Carlo Alberto of Savoy, ruler of Piedmont; in the Second War of Independence (1859), the Savoy Kingdom, allied with France, fought against the Austrian troops to liberate Lombardy. This war ended with the Peace of Zurich on November 10–11, 1859. Under the terms of the peace treaty, Austria ceded Lombardy to France, which, in turn, assigned it to the House of Savoy, but kept Veneto and the border fortresses of Mantua and Peschiera. The Third War of Independence (1866) was fought as part of the much broader Austro-Prussian War and ended, thanks to Austria's defeat by the Prussians, with the annexation to the Kingdom of Italy, of Mantua, and most of Veneto, while Trentino, Eastern Friuli, Venezia Giulia, and Dalmatia remained under Austrian control.

Despite having waged three wars against each other in less than twenty years, in 1882 Italy and Austria concluded an Alliance, which Italy needed above all to ensure a period of peace and concentrate on the consolidation of the newly established State.[7] The limits of the treaty emerged at the outbreak of the Great War, when the opposing interests of Rome and Vienna prevented Italy from joining the war alongside its allies. However, the contradictions inherent in a peace treaty with a country with which there were profound reasons for disagreement—such as the question of the "unredeemed" territories, the competition for influence in the Balkans and the control of the Adriatic Sea—had already emerged in the years running up to the Great War. The former president of the Council of Ministers Alessandro Fortis had pointed out how Italy found itself in the paradoxical situation of having to fear only a war with an allied country. There was a similar anti-Italian sentiment in Vienna. Both Chief of Staff Franz Conrad von Hötzendorf and Crown Prince Franz Ferdinand were convinced that another conflict with Italy was inevitable and that it would, therefore, be better to strike first.[8] All these elements obviously greatly soured relations between the two countries. There were grounds for cooperation, especially in trade and economic matters, and a number of Italian diplomats were pro-Austrian,[9] but this was not enough to overcome the profound territorial contrasts.

The same key features of the strategic culture of Liberal Italy were upheld by the Fascist regime, with an even greater focus on *realpolitik* tenets: centrality/unavoidability of war in international relations, negative view of Italy's opponents, readiness to take advantage of its weaknesses or to deny it its rightful position in the community of States, and a positive assessment of the military instrument and offensive strategic actions. This attitude was taken to extremes through an ideological approach.[10]

Under Fascism, war, "for the first time in the history of mankind, [was considered] not just a hard necessity, an ineradicable element of human society, but also right, positive, beautiful, even a value" (Goglia, Moro, Nuti 2006b: 9). Mussolini's opinion of war embodies well this strategic culture.[11] Mussolini was not particularly interested in military affairs, unlike his ally Hitler, who, on the contrary, interfered heavily in military planning and attached a great deal of importance to the technical aspects of conflicts. For Mussolini, war was just an issue relating to power and should be regarded as a manifestation of politics. Guido Conti (2006) highlights how, although Mussolini never showed an interest in the logistical aspects of war, industrial preparation and the other, less "heroic," elements of warfare, he did show a strong interest in the actual use of the military instrument, to the point of taking over the supreme command in the summer of 1940.

A first element that emerges, with regard to Mussolini's opinion on war, is his exaltation of the human factor. He realized that to win a war, highly trained and motivated troops were needed. The army's morale was considered decisive for gaining the upper hand on the battlefield. This conviction was partly based on an opportunistic attitude (Italy lacked the industrial war potential of the other great powers), and partly it was the result of a sincere overestimation of the importance of human factor compared to material conditions. This faith in the human factor determined the importance Mussolini gave to "numbers" as a power factor, whereby, according to the Fascist conception, Italy should be transformed into a nation in arms. After twenty years in power, one of Mussolini's main concerns was to verify whether his regime had been successful in effectively transforming the Italian people into warriors, capable of standing up to and competing with the other European armies.

The importance of the military training of the people stemmed from the fact that war was viewed as a natural event.[12] Mussolini considered it a sort of "test," to which history periodically subjects the peoples and nations in order to determine which ones have the right to aspire to a top-ranking position in the world hierarchy, and which ones are, instead, destined to a subordinate role. In an essay, dating to the 1930s, he writes that only "war can heighten the tensions of all human energies and impress a seal of nobility on the peoples endowed with the virtues needed to engage in it. All other tests are but surrogates, which do not require man to confront himself in the alternative between life and death" (quoted in Conti 2006: 132).

This vision, however, did not translate into a warmongering attitude. Mussolini claimed that he was a peace lover. But at the same time, with a typically realist style, he believed that a State that wishes to ensure peace and security must prepare to fight with any means. When events precipitated and World War II broke out, Mussolini was deeply convinced that Italy should take the chance of redesigning the political map of the Old Continent.

He had a zero-sum view of the relationships with his opponents.[13] While the Austro-Hungarian Empire had been the principal enemy of Liberal Italy, during the Fascist period this role was played by France and Great Britain.[14] From the start of his political career, Mussolini had been convinced that Italy should escape the narrow confines of the Mediterranean. Given that energy and food resources passed through the Straits of Gibraltar and the Suez Canal, it was essential for Italy to break the French and the British encirclement that was based on the strongholds of Malta, Biserta and Toulon (Knox 1991: 296).

Relations between Rome and Paris soon became strained. In the 1920s, when Paris occupied the Ruhr Basin, Mussolini sympathized with the reasons invoked by the French government to justify this action. After this event, however, the relations between the two countries took a turn for the worse, to the point that, several years later, the Italian ambassador in Paris wrote to Mussolini: "The possibility of war with Italy, which until recently was considered impossible, is now being discussed as a possibility for which France must prepare itself, albeit reluctantly, because this is Italy's desire" (quoted in Mammarella, Cacace 2008: 96).

Various factors were driving the two countries towards conflict. Relations had started to cool in the years after the establishment of the Fascist regime, when the center-left French government had started welcoming the Italian anti-Fascists leaving the country. To this reason — grounded on the ideological and political differences between the two regimes — added differences stemming from territorial claims. Mussolini had put forth claims regarding Tunisia, Corsica, Nice, Savoy, and Djibouti, all territories either under French control, or even a part of France itself. For obvious reasons, France could not meet such huge demands, which would have meant not only redesigning North Africa, political map, but also handing over parts of the homeland.

The relationship with Great Britain was different and, at least until the mid-1930s — at the time of the African Expedition — remained one of mild confrontation, favored, inter alia, by a certain degree of respect enjoyed by Mussolini among British politicians, because of the Italian leader's role in successfully curbing the communist threat. Problems arose between the two countries as a result of Italy's imperialist policy, with Great Britain fearing that Rome's colonial activism could threaten its interests in the Red Sea region.[15]

The Italian government responded to the military measures adopted by the British government to counter the Fascist government's operations in Ethiopia by launching a virulent anti-British campaign, in which Great Britain was depicted as a decadent nation, intent on denying the younger nations their own vital space. This, obviously, further widened the already growing rift between the two countries—fueling negative images in the respective public opinions—and drove Italy into an alliance with Germany. London denounced Italy's action before the Society of Nations and supported the adoption of economic sanctions. From 1937, Mussolini became more and more convinced "that a war of aggression against Great Britain was 'inevitable'" (Knox 1991: 327).

Mussolini's viewpoint was that World War II was a sort of war of religion, fought not just merely for territorial or security reasons, but for asserting and defending opposing principles and ideas. As is always the case when ideas and not material interests clash, Mussolini's viewpoint introduced an element of irreconcilability between the opponents, impelling the Italian leader to further accentuate the aggressive tones of his foreign policy and the stereotyped images of his adversaries. "We cannot go to war without hating our enemies from dawn to dusk, at all hours of the day and night, without propagating this hate and without causing it to become our most intimate essence. We must rid ourselves of all false sentimentality, once and for all" (Mussolini, quoted in Conti 2006: 141).

This image of war as a natural feature of relations between States was accompanied by a positive assessment of the military instrument for attaining political goals. It was considered a "legitimate and necessary means for asserting Italy's independence and equality with respect to the other powers, in the international environment of the Liberal age [. . .] it became a crucial component of the Fascist regime's ideology, which centered its obsessive totalitarian teachings and propaganda on the issues of military preparation and the virtues of war" (Goglia, Moro, Nuti 2006b: 21).

In a declaration to the Chiefs of Staff, in 1927, Mussolini stressed how a strong and quickly mobilizable army was essential to ensure the effectiveness of foreign policy (Minniti 2006: 58). Throughout the Fascist period, there was a constant increase in military spending—in particular to strengthen the navy—for the purpose of supporting the country's international ambitions (table 4.1).

The demographic program itself was aimed, first and foremost, at strengthening the nation's power. Mussolini's fear that by the middle of the century Italy might find itself in a position of inferiority vis-à-vis the other nations encouraged him to sponsor a plan called the "Battle for Births," believing that sixty million Italians could *"bring the full weight of their mass and strength to bear in the history of the world"* (Mussolini, quoted in Knox 1991: 295, original italics).

These traits of the strategic culture fostered a clear preference for offensive military plans. Throughout the Fascist period, strategic planning by the General Staff featured a vast production of offensive military programs (Minniti 2006: 57–62):

Table 4.1 Military spending in Fascist Italy

Year	Spending as a % of the GDP
1923–25	2.6
1927	3.4
1931–1933	5.6
1936	18.4

Source: Knox (1991: 299–300)

- Between 1923 and 1940, no less than twelve strategic plans were developed against Yugoslavia, ten of which were offensive.
- Between 1933 and 1938, defensive plans were prepared to protect Austria, and then offensive plans against Austria and Germany and, between 1938 and 1939, against Germany alone.
- In 1926, an offensive plan was prepared for a possible war with France. This was followed by four defensive military plans towards the end of the 1930s.
- Of the four plans prepared in the second half of the 1930s against Great Britain, one was offensive.

Based on this long list of military operation programs, Minniti concludes that the "number and offensive characteristics of these plans, all of which were applicable, offer a particularly effective indicator of the propensity to war (a different attitude vis-à-vis the determination of declaring it), which intermittently qualified the new power politics of the Fascist government" (Ibid.: 58).

The key points of Liberal and Fascist Italy's strategic culture are summarized in table 4.2.

ITALIAN STRATEGIC CULTURE AFTER WORLD WAR II

World War II and its dramatic aftermath—the heavy defeat, the civil war, the harsh peace conditions—represent a fundamental watershed that led to the emergence of a strategic culture diametrically opposed to that of the previous era. The military defeat favored the emergence of an elite that refused the use of the military force as a means for solving international problems. Regarding this point, Giuseppe Mammarella and Paolo Cacace write (2008: 279):

Table 4.2 – The strategic culture of Liberal and Fascist Italy

Image of war	A natural characteristic of the relations between States
Relations with adversaries	Zero-sum relation
Use of force	Effective
Strategic preferences	1. Offensive actions 2. Defensive actions 3. Accommodation

The dramatic failure of that policy and the national disaster following the military events of World War II marked a historic turning point in the political and existential values of the Italians. The new political forces which alternated in the government of the country held pacifism and internationalism as the core values of their political programs. Those values inspired not only the new Constitution, whose article 11 bans war and commits the national community to supporting the principles and institutions of international cooperation, but also the culture that the nation then accepted and recognized as a defining component of its identity.

The dynamics related to the emergence of a new Italian strategic culture is consistent with Vasquez's explicative scheme illustrated in chapter 2. The assessment of the cost (worth costs/not worth costs) of the last war fought and of its outcome leads to the predominance, in the domestic political milieu, of elites supporting specific strategic cultures, and their greater or lesser stability. As a rule, hard-liners are swept into power by a widespread belief in the utility of war, while accommodationists are preferred if a contrary assessment prevails. Victory generally strengthens the hard-line position; defeat favors the accommodationists' stability (figure 4.1).

The U.S. political elite emerging from World War II (a victorious war seen as worth costs) is an example of an elite supporting a hard-line strategic culture, and strongly rooted in power. Instead, the post–World War I German leadership (that emerged by a war seen as useful, but lost) represents an example of hard-liners with a unstable position in society. The political elites of the United States, France and the United Kingdom after World War I (a victorious war seen as not worth costs) are an example of accommodationists with a shaky position.[16] Finally, the German and Japanese elites after World War II (a war lost at a very high cost) is a case of countries where new governments strongly support a strategic culture grounded on negotiation and the rejection of war.

There are many processes that favor the consolidation of an accommodationist strategic culture.[17] When accommodationists come to power in the aftermath of the disastrous outcome of a conflict that has imposed an enormous cost on society and discredited the strategies preferred by the

**Figure 4.1. Predominance of "hard-liners" and "accommodationists" elites.
Source: Vasquez (1987: 376)**

hard-liners, they try to create a political order and take decisions that make it difficult to resort to the use of force and participate in wars. A strategic culture tends to reproduce and stabilize itself not just through socialization processes, but also through its institutionalization process. This process requires a number of steps (Vasquez 1993: 220–23):

- Creating international organizations for resolving conflicts peacefully, which incorporate antimilitarist ideas. The Society of Nations after World War I and the United Nations (U.N.) after World War II are examples of this process.
- Introducing national laws that make it difficult for a country to participate in a war, as in the case of the postwar constitutions of Germany, Japan, and Italy.
- Establishing rules whereby all other viable instruments of intervention should be tested before resorting to the military instrument.
- Attempting to influence the public opinion, by highlighting the responsibilities of the hard-line supporters for the recent disasters and the negative consequences of the decisions inspired by power politics and nationalist ideas.
- Downsizing military values and the weight of the military in society, by reducing defense spending and the size of the armed forces. Any initiatives aimed at demonizing the role of the defense industry also serve this purpose. Typical, in this regard, is the position of broad sectors of the public opinion and the political elite in 1930s America, during which a committee was established with the task of investigating the responsibilities of the involvement of the Unit-

ed States in World War I. These responsibilities were attributed to the production sectors linked to the arms industry.[18] All these maneuvers lead to cutting back the influence of the military—industrial complex—which is usually allied to the hard-liners—in foreign policy.
- Affirming a nonmilitarized strategic culture is also fostered by the natural inertia of people, that makes mobilization for war purposes very difficult. The greater the disrepute into which the aggressive and warmongering foreign policies of the previous period are brought, the more pronounced this inertia will be. Public opinion will not let itself be easily fired up by nationalistic or interventionist speeches.
- The ensuing bureaucratic implications are that the organizations responsible for managing the foreign policy of a country learn that, for their own "health"—defined in financial, independence and morale terms—it is much better to adjust to the policies set by the supporters of an accommodationist foreign policy. Hard-line persons and organizations will find it increasingly difficult to get their hands on the levers of power and will be less and less successful in the games for the apportionment of the resources.[19] Given the disastrous outcome of a war, even the military will become more wary of supporting aggressive foreign policies or the use of force.

As a result of these factors, at the end of "World War II, accommodationists were dominant in the defeated revisionist States and hard-liners dominant in the victors, who were more status quo oriented" (Ibid.: 223).

All the elements related to the emergence and consolidation of an accommodationist strategic culture are present, to a greater or lesser extent, in the case of Italy. In figure 4.1, Italy is placed together with its former allies (accommodationist/stable).[20] After 1945, due to its heavy defeat in an extremely long, expensive and useless war, a new political elite emerged spearheading a strategic culture that refused many of the characteristics of the previous culture: nationalism, militarism, unilateralism, and offensive strategies.

World War II represented a huge national tragedy for Italy. Not only was Italy beaten on the battlefield, but the consequences and costs of the war proved extremely high: a huge loss of life; high financial costs; heavy institutional repercussions; consequences on sovereignty, with the occupation of the country by a foreign power; loss of the national identity; demotion on the international stage. "The defeat opened a rift between society and the regime. In the space of a few months the consensus enjoyed by Mussolini dissolved and his government began to be seen as the root cause of all the troubles" (Di Nolfo 2006: 238).

The country was left in disarray by the war. About half a million people had lost their lives: over three hundred thousand soldiers and one hundred and thirty thousand civilians. Although the death toll was less severe than in the other two defeated countries—Germany and Japan—where many millions of lives had been lost, it was nevertheless a huge tribute in blood paid by the country for the foreign policy decisions of the Fascist regime. The casualties were less than in World War I, but in 1945 their sacrifice had been pointless, because the country had been defeated and had failed to achieve any of the objectives that had led it into the war. Mussolini had joined the war believing in a rapid victory, which would have enabled Italy to sit at the victors' table,[21] while exactly the opposite occurred. At the ensuing peace negotiations, despite the armistice of September 8, 1943, the country was treated quite like its two former allies.

Economically the consequences were very harsh, too. The infrastructure and factories had been heavily bombed during the five years of war, which had reduced the country to starvation. The gross domestic product had dropped drastically. Taking the year 1938 as a benchmark, in 1945 it had fallen from 100 to 60.7. Inflation in 1946 was 40 percent for wholesale prices and 18 percent for the cost of living. The trade balance was negative by 656.3 million lire. The industrial production indicator, assuming a benchmark of 100 in 1938, had dropped to 87 in 1947.[22] Without aid from abroad there was no way the economy could recover.

To these material consequences of the war, the political and institutional repercussions must be added. The monarchy was in crisis and was finally swept away by a referendum. Even Italy's national identity was heavily affected by the wartime events. The ideas of nation and nationalism, which had been very prominent features of the Fascist ideology, were now discredited and unpopular among the political elites and public opinion. The refusal of the exasperated aggressive Fascist nationalism led to a refusal of the very idea of nation, which, already rather weak, ended up being further diluted after the advent of a party government system, which replaced the former attachment to the homeland through a particularist identification with party's ideology (Rusconi 2005b). The dissolution of the idea of nation resulted in the (often uncritical) adhesion to the international organizations, or in calls for forms of internationalist solidarity.

The costs of the defeat were also measured by the harsh terms of the 1947 peace agreements, under which Italy was basically treated as an enemy State, despite the period of cobelligerence. Between 1945 and 1947, the Italian rulers tried to negotiate a peace treaty that was not too penalizing for the country.[23] Alcide De Gasperi, who became prime minister in 1945 in replacement of Ferruccio Parri and was also acting as Minister of Foreign Affairs, put a lot of effort into achieving this aim. The Italian government's attempts to secure a less harsh treatment met with a certain sympathy by the U.S. president Harry S. Truman, but clashed with the uncompromising attitude of the Soviets, who requested the same treatment for the satellites of Nazi Germany that had fallen under the control of the Red Army. Under these circumstances, the chances that the Italian delegation to the peace conference might obtain less draconian conditions were very slim indeed.

Among the bitter pills the Italian delegation had to swallow, some proved particularly unpleasant, such as those touching the country's territorial integrity. Italy lost sovereignty over certain regions that had arduously become a part of the country thanks to the Risorgimento movement. One of these thorny issues concerned the status of the city of Trieste and its surroundings. On the one side, there was the United States which supported Italy's position, on the other, the hostile attitude of the Soviet Union which supported the claims of Tito over the entirety of Venezia Giulia and even part of Friuli. The break, in 1948, between Belgrade and Moscow further imperiled Italy's position, because Yugoslavia had suddenly become an important pawn to be used against the Soviet Bloc. In the end, Italy lost most of the contested territories, with the only exception of Trieste. Other small territorial concessions had to be made on the western border with France, as compensation for Mussolini's treacherous invasion. Of all the territorial disputes, only the one concerning South Tyrol was resolved in Italy's favor, without any changes to the borders established after World War I.

Equally negative proved the decisions regarding Italy's colonial empire. The diplomatic mission hoped that Italy could keep at least the territories conquered before Mussolini's rise to power (Somalia, Eritrea, and Libya). Here too, however, Rome's hopes crashed against the wall raised by the victorious powers, in this case with the support of Washington, which had always been hostile to colonial expansion. The awarding of a temporary protectorate over Somalia during the process leading to the country's independence was very little in comparison to what had been lost.

The peace treaty also addressed issues such as the war economic reparations and military clauses. As far as reparations were concerned, the Western powers decided to unilaterally waive their rights, being well aware of Italy's serious economic situation. On the contrary, the USSR, Greece, and Yugoslavia insisted in their claims. The military clauses imposed restrictions on the composition and size of the armed forces, with particularly harsh decisions concerning the navy, which was divided among the Allied victors. However, after the peace treaty had been signed the Western powers waived their part, unlike the Soviet Union.

On the whole, the peace terms imposed on Italy were very severe indeed — not dissimilar to those imposed on the other two Axis powers — based on the recognition of Italy's full blame in launching the war. As Mammarella and Cacace write (2008: 156–57): "In short, the treaty not only contained some very harsh punitive clauses, it also strongly condemned post-Risorgimento Italy, sweeping away the illusion — which had long been cultivated by the post-Fascist governments — according to which Mussolini's dictatorship had been a sort of mishap, a mere footnote, in Italy's history." It was no surprise then, that such a traumatic conclusion to the conflict swept away the previous strategic culture—based on power politics—seen by the elites and the public opinion alike as one of the causes of the recent downfall.

A number of decisions taken by the Italian rulers after World War II helped to stabilize the country's emerging nonmilitarized strategic culture. One of these was the forceful support given to the multilateral organizations established in the aftermath of the war in order to curb the use of force in international politics (Ruggie 1997). Right from the start, Italy applied for membership to the United Nations, which was accorded after a lengthy process. The application was filed in May 1947, but due to the opposition of the Soviet Bloc countries, it was rejected a number of times and Rome managed to finally obtain membership only in December 1955. Italy's membership in the United Nations served the twofold purpose of consolidating its regained international status, and anchoring its foreign policy to a multilateral framework, thus marking a radical break with the experience of the Fascist period.

The choice to side with the West, through the membership of NATO, and to build a new Europe, through participation in the European Economic Community, served similar purposes: ensuring security and reconstruction by integrating the country into an international organization that would prevent the reemergence of unilateralist and nationalist tendencies, and consolidating the political orientation of the new political elites as well as anchoring the country to the Western Bloc.[24] The reasons underlying these decisions, of course, also included the Italy's desire of fully recovering its international legitimacy. In particular, the European Community represented an institution conceived to go beyond the discredited logic of power politics. The Community institutions definitely bury the Franco-German rivalry, which had twice devastated the Old Continent, by fostering the creation of what Karl Deutsch (1957) called a "security community": a system of political relations based on the refusal of violent means. In a security community, military force is no longer viewed as a viable option for resolving disputes.[25]

Italy's membership in the Atlantic Alliance, which represented a traditional military alliance directed against an external enemy—as a result of which its ratification encountered a number of obstacles in the left-wing and Catholic parties[26]—enabled the Italian government to free itself from the duty to commit enormous political and material resources for setting up an efficient security system, by delegating this task to other.[27] This allowed the government to focus on more urgent matters, such as rebuilding the economy and consolidating the political institutions.

Alongside the support to multilateral international organizations, the Italian political leaders in the aftermath of World War II chose another path aimed at making it more difficult to wage war in the future: the adoption of a constitution that explicitly refused war as a legitimate means for settling international disputes. The Constituent Assembly had a majority of Catholic, communist and socialist members, who shared, domestically, an anti-Fascist stance and, internationally, a certain convergence on an antimilitarist and internationalist approach. The wording of the constitution was the result of a compromise between these positions. The supporters of ideas more in line with the post-Risorgimento foreign policy were only a small minority. During the works that led to the formulation of the constitution "the pacifist outlook of a people that had been forced — against its will — into a war that it did not want, and that was still under shock due to the devastating consequences of the defeat, was forcefully re-iterated" (Mammarella, Cacace 2008: 159).

The pacifist choice was ratified in article 11 which renounces war as an instrument of international politics and for resolving disputes between States, and establishes Italy's willingness to limit its sovereignty in favor of its full participation in the international organizations. The use of force was envisaged only in the case of defense against an external attack. This was a clear break with the Fascist past and its exaltation of the use of force and of nationalism.[28] In this respect, Italy adopted an approach very similar to that adopted by the other two defeated powers, Germany and Japan (Berger 1996).

The institutional architecture relating to the balance of power between the executive and legislative branches — that tilted towards the latter — was also influenced by the will of the Constituent Assembly to put the Fascist past behind them once and for all.[29] The need to prevent international divisions from causing too great cleavages in domestic politics led the Italian rulers to move the security issues to the back burner, thus removing them from the arena of political competition after the extensive debates on the pro-Atlantic and pro-European choice. An accommodationist strategic culture was consistent with a political establishment that was reluctant to take difficult decisions on issues such as war and the use of military force.

Moreover, in the attempt to further overcome the legacy of the previous regime, politicians and historians attempted to somehow sterilize the twenty years of Fascist rule by emphasizing its episodic nature and the fact that it was altogether alien to the country's political and cultural traditions. This was also aimed at highlighting how Italy's participation in the war was not due to the militaristic nature of the Italian people, or to the pursuit of a national interest according to the classic rules of *realpolitik*, but was the result of a political culture — that of Mussolini's Fascist regime — which did not represent the true spirit of the Italian people.

This strategy also includes the so-called *mito autoassolutorio* (self-justifying myth) with regard to the war crimes committed during the last conflict, which puts forward an image of Italy as a country reluctant to fighting (Focardi, Klinkhammer 2006). As the war operations were scaled down, it became clear that Italian soldiers too had committed war crimes, especially during the Greek and Yugoslav campaigns. Unconventional instruments and tactics had already been used during the colonial wars: the use of asphyxiating gas had debunked the myth according to which Italian colonialism was less brutal than that of the other great European powers.

In January 1944, Benedetto Croce strongly condemned the violent actions committed by the Italian army against the populations of the countries it had invaded. At the same time, however, he underlined how these actions were the result of imitating the behavior of the German troops and were "contrary to the customs and temperament of the Italian people" (Croce, quoted in Ibid.: 252). The philosopher's arguments anticipated one of the themes that were most repetitively used by the Italian government and public opinion in the postwar period, namely that the great majority of Italian soldiers had behaved humanely towards their opponents, avoiding the brutality practiced by other armies.

In the immediate aftermath of the war, for domestic and international reasons, the crimes committed by the Italian troops were hushed up, and the legal proceedings brought against those who had been accused of war crimes generally came to nothing. What emerged, instead, was a war narrative, accepted across the political spectrum and by both the government and civil society, which played down the responsibilities of the Italian military. This was the start of the myth of the "compassionate Italian soldier," which easily became associated with the basic goodness of the Italian people as a whole, reluctant to pursue and glorify any kind of warlike behavior. The worst acts of violence were minimized as either isolated episodes or the activity of fanatical bloodthirsty Fascist squadrons.[30]

The decisions relating to the reorganization of the armed forces were influenced by both the restrictive military clauses imposed by the peace treaty, and the desire to create a completely new army, with no connections to the previous regime. In the first years following the foundation of the Republic, the major concern was not that of an invasion by a foreign State, but the possibility of internal riots and uprisings. The armed forces were therefore organized for the purpose of performing public order duties, rather than serving as a national security instrument. This partly explains the low level of training and inadequate equipment of the soldiers, who, for a number of years, were even fewer in number than the law enforcement officers, and operated as a sort of auxiliary police.[31] At the beginning, the only external security task assigned to the armed forces was preventing sorties by the Yugoslav troops along the border.

The decisions regarding the armed forces were also affected by the broader strategic debate under way within the Western Bloc with regard to where the line of defense against a possible Soviet attack should run. One strategic school of thought held that it was necessary to provide for a forward defense, in which case the front line should pass along the so-called Gorizia threshold. Another school maintained that it would be impossible to resist the Soviet offensive and that Italy should initially be abandoned to the attacking forces and then freed, at a later stage, by means of a counteroffensive launched from Spain. In both cases, the Italian armed forces would receive no particularly demanding duties. In the case of defense of the Gorizia threshold—which was the strategy eventually chosen—the task assigned to the Italian forces was simply to put up a symbolic resistance until the Allied reinforcements arrived, rather than to single-handedly block the advance by the Soviets and their allies. A simple "barracks army," poorly armed and trained, was more than enough to link the country to the Western alliance system. The actual defense of the nation would be guaranteed by the United States.

The choice of a conscription army, besides being the logical consequence of a policy that ruled out particularly demanding external missions for the military, was in keeping with the concern—primarily expressed by the left-wing parties—of preventing the armed forces from becoming too separate from society, as a sort of elite force that could be used by the government for repression purposes or for furthering the ambitions of a single person, as in the case of Mussolini.[32] A particularly significant role, in this direction, was played by the Communist Party (Rallo 1989: 304–5). The communist leaders, in fact, pressed for the democratization of the army. They were strong supporters of "conscription, viewed as a democratic guarantee against any 'pronouncements' by the Armed Forces" (Rochat 1971: 63–64). The Communist Party backed a reorganization of the armed forces in which the internal hierarchical and disciplinary systems served the purpose of ensuring the smooth running of the organizational machine, rather than respect of the hierarchy per se or the perpetuation of military traditions.

In a nutshell, the Italian political establishment, absorbed as it was almost entirely in solving short-term problems, did not pay much attention to military policy.[33] This led to a process of deresponsibilization, or delegation of the military functions (D'Amore 2001: 58–59): on the one hand, the task of ensuring the country's security was outsourced to the alliance system, which basically meant the United States; on the other hand, the political establishment devolved to the military the task of defining the requirements and policies relating to the organization of the defense instrument.[34] Finally, a gap ensued between foreign and military policies, with the latter being dominated by a purely domestic political and bureaucratic rationale, instead of being defined in terms of the country's international objectives.

The decisions taken with respect to the defense industry also contributed to the implementation of a nonmilitarized strategic culture. The military economic sector emerged from the war as shattered as the rest of society. The largest public operator in the sector, IRI (Istituto per la Ricostruzione Industriale), suffered the greatest setbacks. According to the figures reported by Michele Nones (1989: 314), the public-sector shipyards suffered a drop in capacity of about 60 percent. The drop was even higher in the precision mechanics industry, in the region of about 70 percent. Engine production dropped by about 15 percent. The private sector did not fare much better, with FIAT having lost about one third of its fixed assets and Breda in pitiful conditions. Other enterprises too were facing extreme financial difficulties, especially due to the costs for conversion from military to civil activities. One of the hardest hit sectors was the aeronautics industry. According to Defense Minister Randolfo Pacciardi, in 1949 the Italian defense industry featured a gap in technology of at least ten years compared to the other industrialized countries.[35]

To this disastrous situation it should be added another factor that hindered the development of the defense industry: the abundance of American war material on the market at the end of the conflict. This had a twofold negative effect on Italy: it represented an act of unfair competition against the Italian manufacturers, preventing their technological development; and it obliged the Italian military to equip themselves with obsolete armaments that the Americans were getting rid of.

Despite increased military spending, and the economic recovery in the following years, the Italian defense industry continued to lag behind. On the eve of the end of the Cold War, the top fifty defense companies employed a mere 1.3 percent of all manufacturing workers and produced only 1.3 percent of added value (see table 1.1 in Pianta, Perani 1991: 26). As summarized by Mario Pianta and Giulio Perani (Ibid.: 28):

> In short, the Italian military industry is rather small, especially if compared to that of the major European countries [. . .] There is also a general weakness and substantial marginality in the overall production structure of the country. Compared to a generally dynamic industrial system in Italy, the top 50 defense companies feature a lower capacity for growth, with a small and decreasing relevance over the whole manufacturing industry.

These figures reveal a very marginal sector indeed. This impression is further strengthened by the historical series presented by Fabrizio Battistelli, covering a century of military spending in Italy, which reveal a sharp drop after World War II. While military spending accounted for 35 percent of all public expenditure between 1931 and 1940, between 1945 and 1950 it had dropped to 16.4 percent. In terms of GDP, the former accounted for 12.3 percent, the latter for only 3.9 percent (see tables 2 and 3 in Battistelli 1980: 30, 32).

All these initiatives—the membership of international multilateral organizations, the development of a pacifist constitution, the downgrading of nationalism, the rescaling of the military-industrial complex—ended up contributing to the stabilization of a nonmilitarized strategic culture and weakening the supporters of traditional power politics.[36]

In order to more thoroughly describe the characteristics of the strategic culture established after World War II, we must take a look at the orientation of its key supporters: the Catholic and left-wing political forces.[37] Regarding the former, a distinction should be made here between general Catholic thought on war and the ideas expressed by the Christian Democrat leaders.

Christian doctrine is not prejudicially contrary to war. However, war should only be used in a limited number of cases, for defensive purposes. This is the so-called just war theory developed by medieval *Scolastica*. The aim of this theory was to reconcile the moral condemnation of war and the reality of international politics. The solution is a middle-of-the-road position between prowar and pacifist attitudes that identifies a limited number of cases in which the use of force is legitimate. The key tenets of the just war doctrine are the following (Dougherty, Pfaltzgraff 1971):

- A war may be declared only by persons occupying public office. Only persons vested with superior authority have the right to engage in violence against other people. In other words, only States are authorized to wage war. Private citizens are not entitled to use force to uphold their rights.
- A State should engage in war only if it believes that there has been a clear violation of its rights and only after all alternative options have been exhausted. In particular, the use of force must be for defensive purposes only.
- There must be a reasonable expectation that resorting to war shall achieve a positive result. If the damage caused by the use of force would outweigh the ensuing benefits, then no war must be waged, not even in response to an injustice. War waged without taking into account the possible disasters it may cause will only have the result of adding wrong to wrong.
- Once a war has broken out, the two sides must make a proportional use of the military instrument, to avoid any unnecessary damage or suffering to the populations involved. There must be a balance between the means and the ends.[38]

These principles would translate into a series of recommendations regarding the time and place in which wars could legitimately be waged, the prohibition to use certain inhumane weapons and practices, and so on.

The position of the Catholic Church on war, since the beginning of the twentieth century, has been influenced by this middle-of-the-road approach against both abstract pacifism and militarism. In some respects, war is considered a natural element in relations between States, given that, after all, evil does exist in the world. In others, the blame for war is put upon the fact that the society of States fails to conform to the vision of international order supported by Christianity (Moro 2006).

According to Guido Formigoni, the doctrine of the Church in the aftermath of World War II did not rule out a priori the use of force, if dictated by defensive intentions. Fear of the threat posed by the Soviet Union convinced pope Pio XII to "positively consider the strengthening of the West as a way of opposing the communist menace, as a result of which he was not very much inclined towards irenic attitudes. The believers' desire for peace, according to the Christmas radio broadcast of 1948, should be concrete, definitely not 'pacifist.' This approach was suspicious of any form of 'easing of tensions' in the souls, within that great conflict between civilizations represented by the Cold War" (Formigoni 2005: 106–7).

The Catholic Church seemed to escape this ambiguity, and convert from "a prevalent acceptance of the inevitability of war [. . .] to the opposite conviction" (Moro 2006: 401) only after it was faced with the destructive potential of atomic war and the emergence of new international problems as a result of the decolonization process, which shifted the focus from an East/West to a North/South confrontation. This position, moreover, had always been supported by the founder of the People's Party, Luigi Sturzo, who was forcefully critical of the idea of war as a normal feature of international relations, as well as of its legitimacy as a defensive instrument (Ibid.: 385).

The Church's attitude towards war became more decisively condemnatory after the Second Vatican Council. In the encyclical *Pacem in terris*, Pope Giovanni XXIII strongly condemned nuclear weapons and called for their destruction; furthermore, he declared that it was a mistake to consider that war could be used as a means to resolve disputes. A few years later, in his address to the United Nations in October 1965, Pope Paolo VI called for an outright ban on war (Ilari 1986: 242).

The influence of Catholic doctrine on the Christian Democratic (DC) party was rather ambiguous, because the party had many factions, each with a different view of international politics and the role of war: some factions were more ideological, others more pragmatic.[39] Initially at least, the party adopted a rather simplistic and ideological approach to international issues. Since they shirked foreign policy issues, the party leaders tended to rather uncritically adopt the Church's positions. According to Formigoni, this approach translated, between the two world wars, into a Guelph-like position, in which Italy was considered a Catholic nation that should uphold and spread a message of peace throughout the world and act as a mediator in conflicts.

This "inattention" towards international politics disappeared after World War II thanks to De Gasperi. Military defeat, Europe's loss of international clout, and the onset of the Cold War were events that defined the boundaries within which the Italian statesman operated. "Of course, this did not entail a total overhaul of the previous approach, but a profound revision, which led to a new attitude" (Formigoni 2005: 98). During De Gasperi's leadership, the Christian Democratic party maintained a peculiar approach to foreign policy—inspired by the previous tradition—which prompted it to endeavor to iron out international differences and play a role of moderation. However, alongside De Gasperi's pragmatic approach, a more intransigent current of opinion developed, spearheaded by Giuseppe Dossetti, who called for greater independence of the Italian policy from the United States and its military policy, and more sensitive to the pacifist ideals.

After De Gasperi, the Christian Democrat approach to international affairs maintained its original elements, although it grafted them onto a low-profile policy grounded on several key elements (Ibid.: 101–2):

- The relationship, fundamental for security reasons, with the United States and NATO.
- A pro-European stance.
- The attempt to conduct an independent foreign policy towards the Third World countries.
- Support of multilateral international institutions.
- A preference for the use of political instruments in handling conflicts, so as to avoid military escalation.

The coexistence of an ideological and a more pragmatic/opportunistic approach towards international issues resulted in a certain degree of inconsistency in the foreign policy line of the DC.[40] Formigoni distinguishes three factions in the party: the first, that is, the "Orthodox Atlanticist" position, which was espoused by politicians such as Antonio Segni, Paolo Emilio Taviani, and (at least initially) Giulio Andreotti, perceived the choice of belonging to the Western Bloc as not just a security calculation but also a wider question of identity. The Soviet threat made it necessary to join NATO, but the values and cultural traditions that Italy shared with other allies made it necessary, too.[41]

The so-called Neo-Atlantic wing, which comprised men such as Giovanni Gronchi, Amintore Fanfani, and Enrico Mattei, stood in partial contrast to this current. This faction did not question the country's international position but laid claim to greater autonomy in the promotion of the national interest, above all in relation to its dealings with developing countries on which Italy depended for its energy supply. This faction shared some of the positions of Giorgio La Pira, which centered on the need to transcend the logic of the Cold War and to increase international détente, with Italy acting as a conciliator.[42]

Finally, there was the so-called Morotea faction of Aldo Moro. Initially, Moro was not particularly interested in world politics, and he mainly acted in support of Fanfani's initiatives. However, from the end of the

1960s on, his position became more clarified, and he developed a more markedly defined foreign policy. He aimed to move beyond the logic of Blocs by recognizing the growing interdependence of nations and the need of more collegiality in dealing with international issues, thereby removing them from the tight grip of the superpowers. There was a partial convergence between the positions of this faction and the more radical positions held by the left of the party reunited in the "Base." According to Moro, changes at the international level had to be linked to the possibility of triggering deep changes in the internal politics of the country.

Communist thinking on war and peace is in some ways similar to that of Christian doctrine. Both accept the concept of just war: in Christian doctrine, the war of self-defense is just, whereas for Marxists, the struggle of exploited classes against their exploiters (and of oppressed nations against their oppressors) is just. However, war is not inevitable in Marxist philosophy because it is seen as neither the result of an immutable international system (as it is in the realist theory of anarchy) nor the result of man's innate wickedness. War is the product of a particular socioeconomic system—the capitalist system—and as such can be prevented through the abolition of the exploitation of men by other men and of poor countries by rich countries.[43]

From the Marxist point of view, wars are waged by capitalist States and are simply the political expression of the economically dominant classes, which invoke military action to protect and promote their interests. Expansionist foreign policies and international conflicts are the product of the mechanisms and contradictions of the capitalist mode of production in its mature phase. The outward expansion of capital is one of the possible remedies to the recurrent crises: it is a tool for cutting the cost of the production factors and solving domestic situations of overaccumulation. Societies, constantly threatened by the contradictions of the economic system, look abroad for a solution to their internal problems. Capitalists move to conquer markets worldwide, and in so doing they ask for support and assistance by their governments, to defeat their competitors or defend their position. The international system is consequently transformed into an arena where harsh political and military clashes take place. Capitalist countries fight each other to control the world markets, and against the peripheral regions, which they want to transform into political and economic satellites. In the aftermath of World War I, however, there had been some important exceptions among the Marxist theorists of the Second International, like Karl Kautsky, who maintained that imperialist countries could also settle their disputes by means of agreements and therefore avoid unleashing wars for economic reasons.

After World War II there was an initial phase in which the idea still prevailed, in orthodox communism, that war between capitalist and socialist States was inevitable. However, as a consequence of Kruschev's thawing process (that was largely determined by the awareness of the danger represented by atomic weapons), this phase was followed by another one dominated by the idea that conflict between the two Blocs was not inevitable and that peaceful coexistence was possible.

The belief system of Italy's left-wing parties about war reflected both an ideological approach to war and a great deal of opportunism linked to a responsiveness to the new Soviet political course. In the case of the Italian Communist Party (PCI) and the Italian Socialist Party (PSI), this latter being largely dominated, after the war, by the international positions of the former,[44] ideological factors were a very important drives of foreign policy. The two parties shared Marxist-Leninist roots, and throughout its history Italian socialism has been strongly antimilitarist. Military spending was seen as a form of unproductive consumption that could reduce the capitalist system's tendency towards overproduction.[45]

Alongside the ideological factor, the relationship with Moscow played a large part in the development of both parties' political positions. In the 1930s, proletarian internationalism was replaced by the strict observance of the directives emanating from Moscow, which tended to replace the general interests of the working classes with the national interests of the guiding country, i.e., the USSR. This explains the acceptance, by the European communist parties, of the alliance between Nazi Germany and the USSR. In the immediate aftermath of World War II, these parties gradually lost their internationalist features as they changed into national parties striving to win power through the electoral process. This too was partly a result of the political changes decided in Moscow.

All these elements, albeit not always perfectly integrated, can be found in the political culture of the PCI (Aga Rossi, Zaslavsky 2005: 118):

> Therefore, the political culture of the Italian left wing was founded, in those years, on two co-existing, yet often contrasting, elements. On the one hand, the Marxist-Leninist orthodoxy, with the full acceptance of the principal Marxist tenets: the class struggle as the motor of history, and violence as the midwife of revolution, and the prospective collapse and the final clash with capitalism. On the other hand, the characterization of the party as a party qualified to govern the country, with solid roots in Italian society; a party which, therefore, accepted the prospect of forming an alliance with the bourgeois parties and, in particular, the Christian Democrats.

As far as international strategy was concerned, this attitude translated into the refusal of capitalist wars and the acceptance of revolutionary wars. This strongly antimilitaristic attitude was almost always aimed at the wars waged by the United States and the Western countries. Anticapitalism was synonymous with anti-Americanism. Against this backdrop, it can also be viewed the development of a pacifist movement within the left-wing forces, hegemonized by the communists and closely linked to the campaign launched by Stalin for the creation, in Western countries, of forces opposing U.S. military policy. For Moscow, there was a distinction to be drawn between indiscriminate pacifism, which abhorred all war equally, and true pacifism, which condemned the warmongering of the capitalist countries. From this point of view, disarmament campaigns often acquired a unilateral connotation, as they were uniquely campaigns against the Atlantic Alliance's choices.

This attitude justified opposition to NATO—seen as a militarist organization—and to Italy's possible membership of the same. The mobilization against the Korean War had a similar political meaning. According to Elena Aga Rossi and Victor Zaslavsky, the Communist Party was particularly clever in this respect, managing to spread its pacifist concepts even among intellectuals and exponents of the Catholic circles.

The shift from unilateral to universal pacifist culture coincided with the changes produced in 1968 by the Czechoslovakian crisis (the Soviet invasion and the declaration of the "Brezhnev Doctrine"), and was a by-product of a more general cooling in relations between the PCI and the USSR (Pons 2005). After the invasion of Czechoslovakia, the leadership of the PCI began a slow process of separation from Moscow and started developing a new attitude towards international relations. This led to the rift with the Soviet Union in the mid-1970s, and the acceptance by the PCI of the European Community and the Atlantic Alliance. Regarding the issues of war and peace, which previously mingled in the anti-imperialist battles, they were now addressed in more general terms and the "old ambiguity between pacifism and classism dissolved into a new pacifism based on the notion of an interdependent world" (Ibid.: 131). According to Silvio Pons, this new political culture espoused by the PCI centered on three pillars:

- Refusal of the East/West confrontation.
- Acknowledgement of the destructive potential of nuclear weapons and, therefore, of a common destiny of all mankind, beyond the ideological camps.
- A reformist approach.

An "absolute pacifism and the prejudicial rejection of the use of force" thus emerged (Ibid.: 132). However, a certain unilateral pacifism did survive the disappearance of the Soviet Bloc, as a result of which, even today, many antimilitarist positions are characterized by a remarkable degree of anti-Americanism (Aga Rossi, Zaslavsky 2005: 124–125).

If we shift our attention from the image of war and force to that of the adversary, which during the Cold War was the USSR, a complex web of negative and positive views emerges. Although it can be taken for granted that the PCI, and for some time the PSI, did not see the USSR as an enemy, it is also true that Christian Democrat governments also began to demonstrate a more constructive image of the USSR after the period of détente initiated by Khrushev in the second half of the 1950s. They saw the USSR no longer as an adversary but more as a possible source of opportunities.[46]

Domestically, this change in attitude towards Moscow matured in unison with the development of the Neo-Atlantic faction in the governing elites. While remaining loyal to the NATO, the new foreign policy aimed at obtaining more room for Italy to maneuver. One of the areas in which a greater degree of autonomy was sought was that of the relations with the countries on the other side of the Mediterranean, another was that of the relations with the socialist Bloc. This change of policy with regard to the Soviet Bloc countries could be observed in all Western nations, not just Italy, which, however, was capable of taking advantage of the inherent economic and political potential. President Gronchi, a firm supporter of the center-left political coalition, based on the PSI entering the government, showed a certain sympathy towards the East European countries. The Italian leadership no longer saw the USSR as an archrival, with which the only possible interaction was the use of force.

The reasons for intensifying relations with the socialist world were both political and economic: in the former case to carve out a role of mediation between the two Blocs, and thus contribute to the process of détente, and in the latter case to exploit the opening of the markets in the Warsaw Pact countries. To achieve these objectives, Rome and Moscow made strenuous efforts to iron out the last remaining issues from World War II, which still hindered the full normalization of relations: the war reparations, and the fate of the Italian soldiers missing in action during the Russian campaign.

This positive view of the USSR grew stronger during the Gorbachev years. The influence of Gorbachev's coming to power on Italy's attitude towards the USSR is well expressed by former diplomat Roberto Gaja: (1995: 243):

> Above all, it must be recognized that Gorbachev was most likely more popular in Italy than in any other country. It is easy to understand this being the case for Italian communists [. . .] But it was so particularly for the government and the Christian Democrats. The "star wars" era had caused a lot of problems to the Christian Democrat leadership, which had found itself in an uncomfortable position, caught as it was between the defense requirements of the Alliance and the Pope's condemnation of the use of military means, and especially of nuclear weapons [. . .] Gorbachev, therefore, freed the Christian Democrats from a nightmare situation [. . .] Moreover, Italian big industry, which had always had an inclination for the Soviet Bloc, supported a rapprochement with the Soviet Union.

Former Ambassador Sergio Romano also argues that Italy was the country that had the most deep faith in Gorbachev's political turnabout (Romano 2002: 234).

Ideas regarding war, the enemy and the use of military force translated into preferences for different strategic options. Postwar Italian strategic culture prioritized diplomacy as a means to solve conflict. When choosing between offense and defense, defensive strategies were preferred to offensive strategies, in contrast to the Liberal and Fascist periods.[47]

The definition of the strategic options was influenced by the legacy of World War II and by Italy's membership of the Atlantic alliance, as well as by the evolution of NATO's strategic concept regarding the use of the nuclear power. Both these experiences were filtered by the antiwar attitude developed by the policy-makers. Hence, war was seen as a viable option only in a defensive/multilateral framework, in response to an attack. Given Italy's geopolitical position, this led to the elaboration of a security policy centered on the defense of the country's northeastern border.

The various circulars that have been published by the army's General Staff reflect these basic concepts. In the first thirty years of the Republic, four series of documents dealing with the role of the army were published: series 3000, 600, 700 and 800.[48] The first series (3000) still reflected a World War II concept of war and was based on predictions of a typical conventional conflict.[49] The next two series (600 and 700) were issued to account for the nuclear turn in the United States' policy in the 1950s (the strategy of "massive retaliation"). Series 800 was formulated to account for the reshaping of nuclear policy (determined by NATO's shift from "massive retaliation" to "flexible response").[50]

Regarding the choice between offensive and defensive actions, Italian military thought was unquestionably in favor of the latter option. Also as far as the use of tactical nuclear weapons was concerned, the operational doctrine series 600 clearly emphasized the advantages of defense. The doctrinal debate also took into account the possibility of maneuver warfare and of offensive strategies, but, as emphasized by General Filippo Stefani, this was more a theoretical exercise for defining the possible threats to be faced, rather than actual operational options for the Italian army (Stefani 1989: 156).

The preference for defensive action is confirmed by the navy and air force's operational doctrines.[51] The Italian Navy had been severely limited by the clauses of peace treaty after World War II, as it was forced to cede part of its fleet to the victorious countries and was prevented from building up any combat units for offensive purposes. In the various phases that marked the rebuilding of a national fleet and witnessed the gradual substitution of units equipped with the most up-to-date technology for old prewar ships, military planning was always focused on defense. At first, when the only ships in the Mediterranean were those of allies, the naval operational doctrine only allowed for the defense of the Italian coast on the border with Yugoslavia and for the escort of convoys in the case of a conflict with the USSR. The modernization programs launched in the 1950s revealed this underlying general approach, according to which the primary task was "to create a modern 'escort' force" (Ramoino 1989: 189). Even if in the following years—with the gradual withdrawal of the French and British fleets from the Mediterranean, and the menacing appearance of the Russian fleet—the strategic framework became more complex, the principal missions of the Italian navy continued to be fundamentally defensive, in collaboration with the other Western fleets.

As had been the case with the other two services, Italy's membership of NATO was essential for the air force to overcome the constraints imposed upon it by the peace treaty and to initiate a program of modernization. Whereas the air forces of other nations were assigned strategic tasks, Italy's air force was entrusted with the tactical support of ground troops and air defense (Arpino 1989: 211). Over the next two decades, little changed, and despite international developments and improvements in weapons systems technology, defense and tactical missions continued to be at the center of the air force's operational planning. Such priorities were more in line with the thinking of General Amedeo Mecozzi, who was strongly against the offensive use of the air force, than that of General Giulio Douhet, who was a theorist for the offensive role of air power between the World Wars (MacIsaac 1986).

The most striking features of the Italian strategic culture, which emerge from the interweaving of different political cultures (primarily Catholic and Communist) with the pragmatic calculations of politicians, can be summed up in the words of three historians who have studied these issues in detail (Goglia, Moro, Nuti 2006b: 22):

> The Republican age appears [. . .] to be largely characterized by a culture of peace and, indeed, by heated public debate (the case of the socialist/communist campaigns and the Christian Democratic polemic in response is typical) about it. Merely a remnant of a past to be quickly forgotten, war was expressly rejected in the Constitution, while the entire issue of the military and defense endured a long process of delegitimization which led to even research on the subject being regarded with suspicion. After WWII, public opinion, politicians and Italian political culture (whose role in influencing foreign policy became especially important, as in the case of the beginning of détente, or of the bitter debate around nuclear weapons within NATO) were increasingly drawn towards rejection of the war. They insisted on the primary importance of international cooperation and opted, if not for pacifism, for a systematic policy of mediation and of peace (not without, however, a degree of instrumentalism).[52]

The end of the Cold War triggered a reexamination of the Italian security policy (Foradori, Rosa 2007a). It impacted on the propensity to use military force. This has occurred without straying from a defensive-based approach, and especially by carving out an important role for the Italian armed forces in the increasing number of peacekeeping and peace-building missions, which have eventually provided a link between the antimilitarist approach and the growing use of the military instrument.[53] This has not led to any substantial change in strategic culture. The political elites have tried to respond to the new threats and opportunities that have emerged after the fall of the Berlin Wall in 1989 while remaining within the limits (although occasionally stretching them considerably) defined by the postwar strategic culture.[54]

The strategic culture model outlined in this chapter is summarized in table 4.3. In the next chapter I will try to show the consistency between this model and the international behavior of Republican Italy.

Table 4.3 The strategic culture of Republican Italy

Image of war	A historically determined phenomenon not inherent in international relations
Relations with adversaries	Positive-sum relation
Use of force	Effective only in strictly limited cases
Strategic preferences	1. Accommodation 2. Defensive actions 3. Offensive actions

NOTES

1. After its fall in 1943, the Fascist Regime reorganized in the north-central region of Italy as the *Repubblica Sociale Italiana* (1943–1945).

2. Gian Enrico Rusconi reports how the idea of sending troops to the Rhine was accepted by all the principal leaders of the armed forces (Rusconi 2005a: 39)

3. The text of Gen. Cadorna's plan is given in Rusconi (2005a: 155–56): "Summary memo relating to a possible offensive against the Austro-Hungarian monarchy during the current European conflict [. . .] a great battle in Austrian territory, in two or three halts from the border, within 15 days from the offensive; a second battle in six-seven halts from the border within 45 days, for the 3rd and 2nd Armies and the Carnia area and penetration for the 1st and 4th Armies."

4. Chiefs of Staff Command–Office of the Chief of Staff of the Italian Army, *Attacco Frontale e ammaestramento tattico (Frontal assault and tactical instructions)*, circular no. 191 of February 25, 1915, Rome. The document is available at: http://www.icsm.it/articoli/documenti/docitstorici.html. Hereinafter quoted as the: Chiefs of Staff Command 1915.

5. On Italy's colonial wars, see Miege (1976).

6. The following political portraits of the key Italian liberal policy-makers have been taken from Chabod (1965: ch. 2).

7. As Enrico Serra writes (1990: 51): "Salvemini was unquestionably right when he maintained that the Triple Alliance had mostly a 'negative' meaning for Italy because,

in exchange for relinquishing its freedom of action for five years, it obtained a sort of truce from the most dangerous among its possible adversaries, Germany and Austria-Hungary, which undertook not to wage preventive war for the question of Rome and the Unredeemed Territories."

8. "Austria-Hungary [. . .] was firmly convinced, with some reason, that it had never been defeated on the battlefield by the Italian Armed Forces. This fact fueled the suspicion that, sooner or later, Vienna would be tempted to launch a preventive surprise attack against Italy (as suggested by the Chief of Staff General Conrad von Hötzendorf in 1908 to Emperor Franz Joseph on the occasion of the Messina earthquake)" (Santoro 1991: 121).

9. This pro-Austrian position descended from the recognition of the Habsburg Empire's civilizing and stabilizing role over many centuries, and from the hope that the question of the "unredeemed" territories could be solved diplomatically (Monzali 2005: 25–26).

10. Regarding the points of contact between Realism and Fascism, see Randall Schweller (2009: 237): "Fascists and Realists shared many core principles about the nature of world politics, the role of the modern State, and the maximization of national power through territorial expansion."

11. This section draws from Conti (2006).

12. See the item *guerra* (war) in the *Grande Dizionario Enciclopedico* published by UTET in 1935 under the supervision of the historian Pietro Fedele, former Minister of Education from 1925 to 1928: "War, therefore, is a state of fact which nations use, out of historical necessity and biological instinct, to affirm a right or protect an interest, relying on force and violence" (vol. 5: 1127).

13. This attitude could already be seen before he conquered power in 1922. As Renzo De Felice writes (1974: 333): "it can be said that international relations were already viewed by him under a Darwinistic light, so to speak, with regard to both the life of peoples and States and the power relations that determined and governed them. For Mussolini *imperialism* was the 'eternal and unchangeable law of life.'"

14. Italy's enemies were the "exquisitely plutocratic and bourgeois" nations (Mussolini, quoted in Knox 1991: 296).

15. Mussolini had already expressed his interest in dismantling the British Empire in 1922 (Knox 1991: 296).

16. In Italy, in the aftermath of World War I—a war that was won and, albeit at a very high cost, was considered useful for the attainment of national interest objectives (Rusconi 2005a)—the disappointment for the "halved victory" sanctioned by the Peace Conference of Versailles strengthened the hard-line position, favoring the rise to power of Mussolini, who supported a nationalist, expansionist and aggressive foreign policy.

17. Actually, Vasquez does not expressly speak of strategic cultures, but of the practices followed by the political elites. However, his way of intending the domestic foundations of foreign policy decisions overlaps with the concept of strategic culture. As previously mentioned, the concept of culture in this work refers to the practices learnt by the members of a certain society about how to tackle certain problems. Henceforward, I will use the expression "nonmilitarized strategic culture" to refer to the orientations of an accommodationist-dominated leadership.

18. The "Nye Committee [. . .] in 1934–1936 investigated on behalf of the United States Senate the influence of the financial and industrial interests on the intervention of the United States in the first World War. The publicity which the proceedings of this Committee received made the 'devil' theory of imperialism for a time the most popular explanation for foreign affairs in the United States. The simplicity of the theory contributed much to its popularity. It identified certain groups that obviously profited from the war, such as manufacturers of war materiel (the so-called 'munitions makers'), international bankers ('Wall Street'), and the like. Since they profited from war, they must be interested in having war. Thus war profiteers transform themselves into

the 'warmongers,' the 'devils' who plan wars to enrich themselves" (Morgenthau 1948: 46).

19. The political and bureaucratic dynamics are affected by the predominant climate in a society. The various players participating in the foreign policy-making process tend to take the predominant political climate into account, in order to position themselves accordingly. As Werner Schilling writes (1962: 96) in respect of the formation of the U.S. defense budget in 1950: "[. . .] members of the Executive and Congress start their thinking about the budget with a common and very narrow range of figures in mind. The area of their choice is closely limited by the prevailing climate of opinion regarding desirable and possible defense budgets [. . .] Secondly, the particular choices made by the members of the Executive and Congress within the limits set by the climate of opinion are not made in intellectual isolation and independence. They are, instead, strongly pre-conditioned by a sense for what the other members want or will do."

20. Regarding Germany and Japan, see chapter 3.

21. "The war was a means by which Fascist Italy, allied with Nazi Germany, would have accomplished the dream of grandeur the regime had so fondly caressed [. . .] the necessary means for achieving the goal the Italian establishment had aimed to since the creation of the kingdom: to make Italy a 'great power,' not just in name, but in reality as well, because this would have enabled it to dominate the Mediterranean, rebalance power relations in Europe and carry out a power politics that would have driven the Italian economy" (Di Nolfo 2006: 230, 232).

22. All the figures have been taken from the website of the Bank of Italy: http://www.bancaditalia.it/statistiche/storic/collanastorica.

23. The following paragraphs regarding the peace treaty are based on Mammarella, Cacace (2008: 150, sgg), Romano (2002: ch. 1), Varsori (1998: ch. 1).

24. Regarding membership of NATO and the European Community, see Graziano (1968: cap. III), Barié (1988), Varsori (1998: chs. II, III).

25. For an analysis of the Italian Europeanist thought and its conception of federalism as an instrument for overcoming, once and for all, the bellicose rationale of the European interstate system, see Graglia (2006).

26. The Communist Party's opposition was taken for granted, but opposition by certain factions in the Christian Democratic and Socialist Parties came as a surprise. "As mentioned previously, there was the opposition of certain left-leaning Christian Democrats, like Giovanni Gronchi, who insisted that Italy should remain outside both military blocs; there were the members of the 'Politica sociale' group and the so-called 'professorini' [young professors], supporters of Giuseppe Dossetti, including the young Undersecretary of State for Foreign Affairs Aldo Moro; there was the creeping opposition of a large sector of Saragat's party which, during a meeting of the party's leadership, voted in a majority against Italy's membership of the Atlantic Alliance, although the parliamentary group then overturned this decision" (Mammarella, Cacace 2008: 179).

27. As mentioned by Silvestri (1990: 185): "In defining the strategic decisions of the Atlantic Alliance in Europe, several analysts have coined the expression 'defense on the cheap' [. . .] which is well suited to the case of Italy." As concerns the consequences of Italy's decision to join NATO, Carlo Jean writes (1990: 146): "Undoubtedly, instead, membership of NATO led to a loss, in Italy more than elsewhere, of the 'national' dimension of the culture of security and defense".

28. As Laura Forlati Picchio writes (1988: 439): "Article 11 contains a political message intended to convey, to the allied and associated powers emerged victorious from World War II, the solemn repudiation—by the newly formed Italian Republic—of the former regime, and of the foreign policy associated with it."

29. "To prevent the return of any authoritarian regime, Italy gave itself a government with few powers and easily controllable by the parliament" (Dottori, Gasparini 2001: 51).

30. "The image of the 'bad German,' a fanatical warrior capable of committing any evil, was countered by that of the 'good Italian.' Badly equipped and catapulted, against his will, into a wretched war, the Italian soldier purportedly sympathized with the local populations, easing their burden of hunger and misery, sharing with them the little he had, and, above all, protecting them from the abuse and violence of the Germans troops" (Focardi, Klinkhammer 2006: 266).

31. "The geographical deployment of the regional commands, concentrated in the Po basin and on the Appennines, as well as the characteristics of the military exercises in the period, and the regulations governing intervention for public order purposes, highlight the Army's prevailing internal security functions" (D'Amore 2001: 54).

32. Regarding this point see chapter 3, relating to the studies by Kier on the relationship between military format and political party orientations.

33. "With national assets down by about one third compared to 1938, the national income halved, reduced tax revenue as a result of both the drop in income and the effects of inflation, the first phase of postwar politics was entirely focused on coping with emergency in the food sector, the electricity industry, transportation and other sectors of vital importance. In these conditions, we can easily imagine how little resources there were to support State policies, national defense included" (Mayer 1989: 275).

34. "For years nothing was said about it, due to excessive repugnance and fear about the possible political use of military force" (Santoro 1991: 281).

35. Statement by the Minister of Defense to the Chamber of Deputies on September 27, 1949 (quoted in Nones 1989: 317).

36. Jennifer Lind (2004) questions whether the security policy of Tokyo is based on utilitarian considerations of *realpolitik* (to exploit the advantage offered by the American strategic umbrella to achieve security at a low cost), or whether it derives from a pacifist attitude. This dilemma is false because decisions made at time t for opportunistic reasons—such as buck-passing—can be internalized and become normatively determined at time $t+1$ (Johnston 2008). Recurring actions become part of the repertoire of strategies that are considered to be normal by the members of a society when handling particular problems (Swidler 1986).

37. A third group—largely minority in the national political arena but very combative in spreading the peace themes within society from the 1960s—was the Italian Radical Party (Ilari 1986).

38. The last two principles were the most invoked during the debate, in the early 1980s, regarding the immorality of nuclear warfare, incapable of distinguishing between combatants and civilians, and of controlling damage and ensuring victory at an acceptable cost.

39. The following references to the Christian Democratic party are based on Formigoni (2005).

40. Giorgio Rumi argues that the foreign policy of Italian Catholic politicians fluctuated between opportunism and prophecy (quoted in Formigoni 2005).

41. Regarding the importance of "identity" in the construction of the Atlantic Alliance, see Risse-Kappen (1996). He argues that "the Western alliance represents an institutionalization of the transatlantic security community based on common values and a collective identity of liberal democracies. The Soviet domestic structure and the values promoted by communism were regarded as alien to the community, resulting in a threat perception of the Soviet Union as the potential enemy" (Risse-Kappen 1996: 395).

42. In 1952, La Pira organized the *First International Conference for Peace and Christian Civilization*. During the 1960s, he developed a vision of international politics that advocated abandoning the State-centric order and stressed the importance of promoting peace and banning war in order to foster the development of mankind (Ilari 1986: 245).

43. Unlike the realists, who have a pessimistic vision of history, Marxists have a positive attitude, tied to the possibility of changing and improving human beings.

Concerning the belief systems—the operational code—of the communist leaders, see George (1969).

44. According to Aga Rossi and Zaslavsky, the Italian socialist party, in the aftermath of World War II, was entirely in subjection of the communists, for various reasons: because of a sort of psychological submission, and the belief that, eventually, the Soviet Bloc would prevail over the West. In other words, "Nenni felt that he was on the winning side" (Aga Rossi, Zaslavsky 2005: 121). What follows is substantially based on the work of these two scholars.

45. One of the first Marxist analysis of military spending was by Rosa Luxemburg. A contemporary neo-Marxist author espousing a similar approach is James O'Connor.

46. This part on the relations with the USSR is mainly based on Bagnato (2006).

47. The strategic preferences of Republican Italy have been drawn from the employment doctrines of the three military services between 1945 and 1975.

48. Regarding the evolution of the doctrine on the use of land forces, see the writings of General Filippo Stefani (1989).

49. At the beginning, the possession of atomic weapons did not lead to any major changes in the American defense policy. The power of the new devices was not immediately clear. They were considered simply as a new type of arms, much more powerful than conventional arms. Their predominantly dissuasive scope was grasped only gradually, and it was only in 1948 that the principles of nuclear deterrence were formally introduced into the American defense policy (Freedman 1989: 53).

50. The "massive retaliation" strategy, announced by Secretary of State John Foster Dulles in January 1954, was the keystone of the *New Look*, the security policy embraced by President Eisenhower. This approach wanted the United States to retaliate to any attack with a massive and immediate atomic strike against the enemy's territory. "Massive retaliation" was the direct consequence of the strategic superiority of the United States, which in those years could still threaten to launch a first strike without fearing the consequences of a devastating retaliatory blow (Snyder 1962). The "massive retaliation" doctrine was replaced by the "flexible response" strategy in the 1960s. This strategy envisaged a multiplication of the—atomic and conventional—alternatives available to the policy-makers. In the event of a military action by the enemy, there would be no immediate atomic retaliation, but a response commensurate with the assault. The selectivity of the nuclear response was an approach proposed primarily by the Defense Secretary Robert McNamara, not at all happy about the inflexibility and number of civil casualties that the war plan (SIOP) inherited from the previous administration entailed (Rosenberg 1983: 67).

51. Regarding the evolution of the employment doctrines of the navy and air forces, see the writings of Admiral Pier Paolo Ramoino (1989) and General Mario Arpino (1989).

52. The predominance of an accommodationist strategic culture within the main Italian political parties does not contradict Kogan's thesis (1963), taken up by Incisa di Camerana (Garruccio 1982), according to which a persistent trait in the Italian political thought is an almost obsessive focus on the issue of the balance of power in all its manifestations: global, regional, national. The point is, as claimed by Swidler (1986), Kier (1996) and Johnston (1995a), that cultures influence not so much the values, the ends that policy-makers endeavor to accomplish, as the action strategies they use for this purpose. Thus, as Incisa di Camerana writes, this preoccupation with achieving a balance of power was effectively at the center of Italy's international actions in both the Liberal and Fascist periods and the Republican period; what changes radically is the type of response the State gives in the three periods. In the Republican period, war is no longer seen as a feasible option, the military instrument is no longer considered as effective and legitimate, the preferred international strategies are of a diplomatic rather than military nature.

53. I will come back to this point in the next chapter.

54. For a convincing analysis of this issue, see Pirani (2008).

FIVE
Italy's Strategic Culture and International Behavior

In the previous chapter I have illustrated the most significant traits of the Italian strategic culture in the Republican period. In this chapter I will attempt to analyze its impact on Italy's international behavior. From a neorealist perspective, the events of 1989 that led to the collapse of the bipolar system and to the demise of the main threat justifying NATO should have brought about profound changes in the Italian security policy such as:

- Greater assertiveness and a higher international profile.
- An increase in defense spending.
- A weakening of support for international security organizations.
- The emergence of a more marked inclination towards unilateral actions, including military action.

Conversely, one of the assumptions of a cultural approach is that the repertoire of practices comprised in a security culture (and from which actors choose strategies with which to tackle particular issues) is persistent and does not fade away easily. Thus, even when national and international material structures change, policy-makers continue to react to security issues according to procedures deriving from their strategic culture. If we assume that the post–World War II strategic culture, which was consolidated over many years, is still influential, then we should find that even in changed international circumstances, Italy continues to be a country that:

- Uses military force reluctantly.
- Does not invest heavily in weapons.
- Supports multilateral organizations.

- Tends to frame its interventions as peace missions rather than acts of war.

In the following pages, I will test these hypotheses by analyzing a series of themes, including involvement in militarized disputes, patterns of defense spending, and attitude towards multinational security organizations, as well as by reconstructing the main military actions abroad.

ITALIAN BEHAVIOR IN MILITARIZED INTERSTATE DISPUTES

A quantitative analysis of Italy's military behavior allows one to take an initial look at the country's attitude towards the use of force. To do this, I have used data from the *Correlates of War* (COW) project on militarized interstate disputes (MID), which includes the years up to 2001.[1] A militarized interstate dispute is defined as a historical event in which the threat, deployment, or use of force by one state is unequivocally directed at the government, property, or territory of another state (Jones, Bremer, Singer 1996: 168). The level of violence in a dispute can range from simply threatening the use of military force to the declaration of war.[2]

From an initial comparison with other countries, we can see that Italy is not a war-prone state (figure 5.1). Since the postwar period, the United States has been party to almost four disputes per year; China to almost three; the United Kingdom, Russia, and India to almost two and Japan and France to approximately one per year. Germany and Italy only became involved in one dispute every three years. From this viewpoint, these aggregate data are consistent with a nonmilitarized strategic culture.

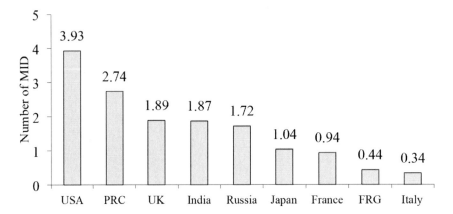

Figure 5.1. Nations' involvement in MID (MID per year, 1946–1992)

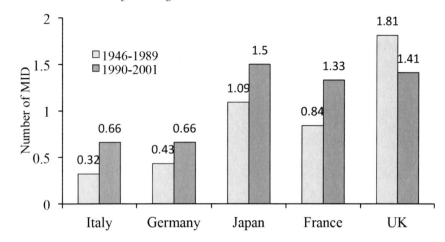

Figure 5.2. Middle Powers' involvement in MID (MID per year, comparison of five nations)

The differences are even more significant if countries, which because of their size, international responsibilities and traditions occupy a particular position in the world (e.g. the United States, Russia, and China) are excluded from the comparison. A comparison among middle-sized powers such as France, the United Kingdom, Germany, Japan and Italy shows that Italy was the country least inclined to be involved in military disputes during the Cold War (figure 5.2). Although the watershed represented by the year 1989 led to a general increase in the use of force, that was most likely caused by the instability generated by the collapse of the blocs and the increased freedom of maneuver gained by medium-sized powers, in line with neorealist argumentations. The fact that Italy and Germany, that is, countries with a nonmilitarized strategic culture, always have the lowest score on the scale (Japan is a partial exception) confirms the idea that, even within a more permissive international climate, an acquired repertoire of cultural practices continued to influence the international behavior of these countries. The pressure exerted by external factors is not enough to explain how a state will behave, since this is affected by how the policy-makers of a country habitually perceive international events and the main intervention strategies.

We see little change when moving from a cross-national comparison to a longitudinal one. I have evaluated four subperiods in Italian history: the Liberal period, from the foundation of the unified state to the advent of Fascism (1861–1921); the two decades of Fascism (1922–1943/1945); Republican Italy during the Cold War (1946–1989); and Republican Italy during the post–Cold War era (1990–2001) (figure 5.3). The period that saw the most conflicts was the Fascist period (60 MID, or 2.5 conflicts per year), followed by the Liberal period (41 MID, or 0.67 per year), the post–Cold War period (8 MID, or 0.66 per year) and finally, the Cold War period that has shown the least resort to the use of force (14 MID, or 0.32 disputes per year). These statistics are compatible both with a neorealist interpretation, which refers to international anarchy and Italy's security interests, and with a cultural interpretation. The bellicosity in the Liberal period can be linked to the demands involved in the construction of the new state, which was intended to complete the project of the *Risorgimento* and confirm Italy as a genuine great power, and which ultimately led to Italy's involvement in World War I (Rusconi 2005a). The bellicosity of the Fascist period can conversely be seen more as a result of the strongly militarist tendencies of the regime's strategic culture—as illustrated in the previous chapter—than of any modification in Italy's international position, which in fact remained substantially unchanged (Schweller 2009). Similarly, the constraints on any increase in Italian military activity in the post–Cold War period seem to be more linked to cultural factors, that is, a resistance to adopting *realpolitik* practices, than to structural deficiencies or domestic political reasons.

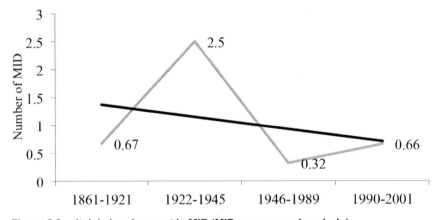

Figure 5.3. Italy's involvement in MID (MID per year, subperiods)

If we combine the four subperiods, then the contrast between the Italy featuring a strategic culture molded by *realpolitik* and the cult of the offensive (1861–1945) and the Italy featuring an accommodationist strategic culture (1946–2001) becomes even more striking. The number of MID in which Italy was involved in the former period is three times higher than that in the Republican period (figure 5.4).

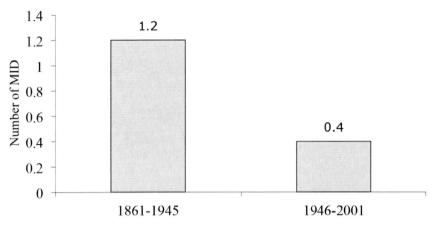

Figure 5.4. Italy's involvement in MID (MID per year, aggregated subperiods)

These data fit neatly into the strategic cultural model but do not necessarily exclude other interpretations. We must consider other aspects of Italy's behavior regarding war to better understand the effects of cultural factors. As mentioned in chapter 3, an important component of strategic culture is the preference for certain operational options, more or less violent, and more or less offensive. The MID project distinguishes five possible levels of violence on a scale from 1 (minimum) to 5 (maximum):

1. Nonmilitary action
2. Threat to use force
3. Display of force
4. Use of force
5. War

By calculating the average level of violence used by Italy (figure 5.5), we see that it tends to decline during the transition from the Liberal to the Fascist period. This tendency becomes even more marked during the Cold War. The post–Cold War period appears to buck the trend, but the data are in fact distorted by the limited number of MIDs: a small number of interventions, with a high level of violence, weigh disproportionately in the calculations of the average level of violence. Out of the eight MID in which Italy was involved in this period, one was a "real" war (the 1991 Gulf War) and two involved the massive use of military force (former Yugoslavia and Kosovo). A gross comparison of the pre and post–World War II periods confirms that Italy was less inclined to use violence in the second period (figure 5.6).

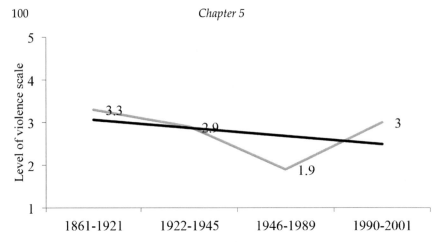

Figure 5.5. Level of violence used by Italy (subperiods, average value)

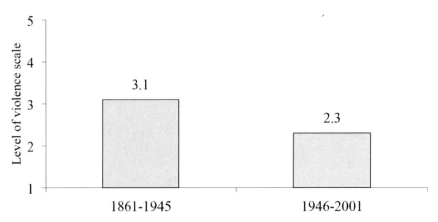

Figure 5.6. Level of violence used by Italy (aggregated subperiods, average value)

A cross-national comparison of the medium-sized powers also shows that countries with a nonmilitarized strategic culture (Italy, Germany, and Japan) tend to resort less frequently to high levels of violence than countries with a "warlike" tradition, such as the United Kingdom and France (figure 5.7). This tendency holds both in the Cold War period and afterwards, which demonstrates that changes in the international system cannot alone explain the differences in these five countries' security policies.

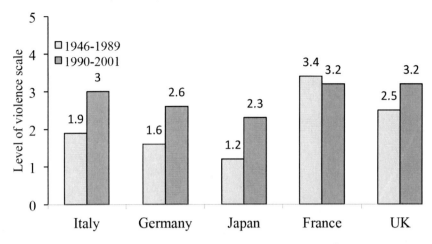

Figure 5.7. Level of violence (comparison of five nations, average value)

We obtain a fuller picture of Italy's military conduct by examining the reasons for its involvement in military disputes. The COW project distinguishes countries that pursue revisionist objectives from those whose policies are intended to maintain a status quo. Although there is no direct link between offensive and defensive strategies and between revisionism and the status quo, it is clear that whereas the status quo can be maintained by both offensive and defensive means, revisionist objectives necessarily imply more offensive actions. The data for Italy show a very marked decline in its revisionist objectives after World War II (figure 5.8). Revisionist objectives were implicated in 19 out of 44 instances (43.1 percent) in the Liberal period and 26 out of 60 instances (43.3 percent) during the Fascist period. During the Cold War, there were no disputes involving revisionist objectives. In the post–Cold War period, 2 out of 8 disputes involved revisionist objectives.

When arranging the four periods into two groups, the difference is remarkable (figure 5.9). In the period characterized by a hard *realpolitik* strategic culture, 45 out of 104 events (43.2 percent) involved revisionist policies. During the years of Republican Italy, 2 out of 22 events (9.1 percent) involved revisionist policies. From these figures, one may infer that the behavior of Republican Italy is much less aggressive than that of the two previous periods.

The *Correlates of War* project differentiates three types of revisionist policies. The first type is based on territory. In this case, the states engage in actions aimed at occupying or recovering parts of the territory and changing national borders. Type two policies are those that involve actions aimed at changing the behavior of another nation. Finally, type three revisionist policies involve policies aimed at overthrowing the political regime of a nation. The diverse distribution of these types of conflicts are closely linked to Italy's construction and national consolidation processes. In the Liberal period, the most pursued foreign policy goals are of type two. In second place are the territorial goals linked to the Italian *Risorgimento* policy. Third place is taken by the policies aimed at changing the political regime of another nation. The trend is quite similar under the Fascist regime, that featured a strongly revisionist foreign policy. In the Republican era, the only disputes implying revisionist goals are of type two, aimed at affecting the adversary's political line.

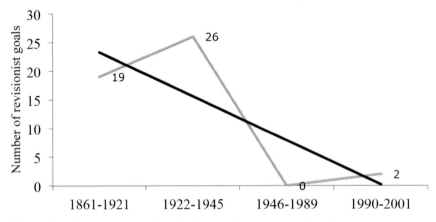

Figure 5.8. Revisionist goals in Italian foreign policy (subperiods)

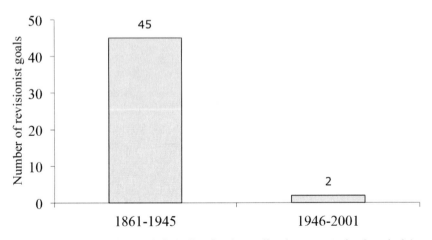

Figure 5.9. Revisionist goals in Italian foreign policy (aggregated subperiods)

One last detail in this reconstruction of Italy's conduct in militarized disputes is provided by an analysis of the types of action used in the pursuit of its objectives. The MID dataset distinguishes among twenty-two different possible types of conflictive action, which enables us to gain a more detailed picture than that provided by the five-item violence scale described earlier:

1. No militarized action
2. Threat of using force
3. Threat of blockade
4. Threat of occupying territory
5. Threat of declaring war
6. Threat of using nonconventional weapons
7. Threat of joining war
8. Show of force
9. Alert
10. Nuclear alert
11. Mobilization
12. Fortifying borders
13. Border violation
14. Blockade
15. Occupation of territory
16. Seizure
17. Attack
18. Clash
19. Declaration of war
20. Use of nonconventional weapons
21. Begining interstate war
22. Joining interstate war

The data for Italy are given in figure 5.10. They show the strategic preferences in the different historical periods, even if a clearly defined model of Italy's conduct does not emerge. In the Liberal period, which was strongly influenced by the need to complete the project of national unity, the government's preferred options were as follows: display of force (13 instances), occupation of enemy territory (8 instances) and war (4 instances, including participation in conflicts started by others and those initiated by Italy itself). In the Fascist period, the preference was for nonmilitary actions (20), followed by military attack (14), displays of force (7) and participation in war (7, considering wars initiated by Italy or joined later). In the Cold War period, the preference was for nonmilitary action (8) and displays of force (4). No discernible model has emerged since the end of the Cold War, given the low number of cases, more or less equally distributed across the possible options. When we consider only the larger conflicts, we see that Italy fought in eleven wars between 1861 and 1945 (approximately one conflict every seven years). The Republican Italy was involved in only one war over a fifty-year period (1945–2001).

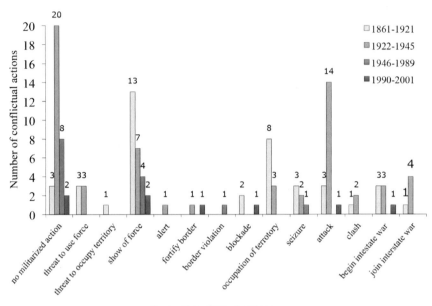

Figure 5.10. Type of conflictual action used by Italy

The facts so far suggest that, in general, Republican Italy was less inclined than the other medium-sized powers (Germany, Japan, United Kingdom, France) to become involved in military disputes. It also tended to resort less frequently to high levels of violence in comparison with other countries and previous historical periods. In the Liberal and Fascist periods, Italy was much more willing to engage in conflict than it was in the first fifty years of the Republic. The fact that Italy rarely resorted to the use of military force even after the Cold War is a strong argument in support of the approach of strategic culture.

To dispel the uncertainties present in the quantitative data, I will now move on to an analysis of Italy's military spending and its attitude towards multilateral organizations. Finally, I will describe in greater detail the major conflicts in which Italy has participated since the end of the Cold War.

ARMED FORCES AND MILITARY SPENDING

As illustrated in chapter 4, the Italian armed forces were restructured in the aftermath of World War II, especially with the aim of maintaining domestic order. Their main external security mission consisted in the static defense of the Gorizia threshold where, in the event of an attack by Warsaw Pact troops, they were supposed to act as a catalyst for the triggering of the intervention of the North Atlantic Alliance. In view of such minimal tasks, not much importance was given to their modernization or operational readiness. Of greater concern than the armed forces' efficiency was their "democratic nature."

As pointed out by Leopoldo Nuti (2006), even more than the limitations on the Italian rearmament imposed by the peace treaty, it was the deep cleavage between citizens and armed forces that favored the rise of a strong antimilitarist feeling that in turn brought about a low-profile defense policy. The very same lobbying of Italian diplomats and government for a revision of the restrictive clauses imposed by the peace treaty should not be interpreted so much as an attempt to obtain the consensus for the development of a stronger military, but rather as an attempt to recover the lost international status and to obtain wider margins to maneuver for Italy's international action. It was more a question of "status" than of operational capacity.

The Atlantic solution to security problems lasted until the late 1960s, when the East-West détente processes (marked by important diplomatic events, such as the signing for the partial ban on nuclear testing in 1963, and the signature, in 1968, of the nonproliferation treaty, NPT) created a bit of disenchantment among Italian diplomats regarding the reliability of America's security commitments. As Nuti writes (Ibid.: 487):

> One must therefore assess the NPT not as a simple development of the complex, byzantine world of the arms control but in its profound political effect: many Italian politicians and diplomats, in fact, saw it as an unequivocal sign of change in America's strategic priorities. Although for many of them the détente was a positive phase in the evolution of the international system, for the advent of which they had fruitfully worked in previous years, it should not have implied America's withdrawal from Europe, not to mention an agreement among superpowers *sur le dos* of the Europeans.

In addition to the nuclear issue, another factor that led to the rethinking of Italy's security policy was the Vietnam War, which fueled the concern that the United States would start to increasingly focus on the Asiatic theatre in lieu of the European one. These concerns resulted in the adoption of a set of special spending laws aimed at modernizing the three armed forces. In the mid 1970s, the Italian Navy, Air Force and Army submitted their priorities for increasing the efficiency of the military. These initiatives were collected in the *White Paper* on defense of 1977 (Perani, Pianta 1992). This was made possible also by the changes in domestic politics, where the advent of the "Historic Compromise" experiment involved the Italian Communist Party's acceptance of a greater role of the armed forces and an increase in defense expenditure.

Another innovation happened in the mid 1980s, when gradual changes in Italy's security policy were made, once again stimulated by international events. Of special importance were the Euro-missile crisis (1979–1983), and Italy's participation in the multinational mission in Lebanon (1982–1984). The latter "indicated a new type of defense policy, less constrained by the Atlantic logic and more linked to the will to use the national military instrument to project influence on a crisis area" (Nuti 2006: 500). The participation in the Lebanon mission allowed the Italian armed forces to restore a positive role within society. For them this was a new type of foreign action, legitimized by the coverage of international organizations and by the mission's pacific purpose.[3]

This increase in activity stimulated a second *White Paper* on defense, published in 1985, which described a new architecture for the armed forces, including the new commitment to peacekeeping missions. The political debate concerning this particular aspect of the *White Paper* is a measure of the significant importance and conditioning exerted by an accommodationist strategic culture. The *White Paper*, presented by Minister of Defense Giovanni Spadolini, subdivided the tasks of the armed forces into five operational missions (Caligaris, Santoro 1986):

- Mission 1: defense of Italy's northeastern and northern borders.
- Mission 2: defense of the southern front and of the Mediterranean.
- Mission 3: air defense and deterrence.
- Mission 4: operational defense of the national territory.
- Mission 5: international security actions.

The first four missions did not show much change from the classical role. They accomplished the tasks for which the three Armed Forces had long prepared, following their reorganization in the post–World War II period. Mission 1 was assigned to the army, Mission 2 to the navy, and Mission 3 to the air force. Mission 4 covered the national security tasks left out by the first three. This mission, according to Santoro, was the most traditional of them all (*Ibid.*: 93):

> The mission "Operational defense of the national territory" is the one closest to the traditional organization of the Italian Armed Forces during the nineteenth century and the prewar period. One could say that it is the continuation of the garrison-army, located in the "Comiliters" and military "Districts," structured for the recruitment and training of conscripts in the state's large and medium-large cities, indirectly in charge of internal deterrence and in some cases of public order.

The most radical change—absolutely revolutionary compared to the organization of the military in previous years—was represented by Mission 5 that envisaged the creation of a rapid reaction force at brigade level, consisting of about then thousand troops, for actions in crisis areas or in low-intensity conflicts. Besides the expectation being to a certain extent unrealistic, due to budget limitations, the project was met with strong political opposition, as it was considered a surreptitious form of force-projection, in contrast with the country's recent history. This led to the "hiding" of this rapid reaction force in the folds of the more traditional and politically acceptable Mission 4.

Italy's low-profile defense policy has had a restraining effect on military spending throughout the post–World War II period. During the 1980s, Italy's defense expenditure was roughly half that of the United Kingdom or France and also considerably less than that of West Germany (table 5.1).[4] The situation did not particularly change after the Cold War. The relative difference decreased not because Italy began to spend more but because other countries were spending less.

Table 5.1. Military expenditure as a percentage of GDP in major European countries

Year	Italy	Germany	France	UK
1980–1984	2.2	3.3	4.1	5.2
1985–1989	2.2	2.9	3.7	4.4
1990	2.1	2.8	3.6	4.1
1991	2.1	2.3	3.6	4.3
1992	2.1	2.1	3.4	3.8
1993	2.1	1.9	3.4	3.6
1994	2.0	1.8	3.3	3.3
1995	1.9	1.7	3.1	3.1
1996	1.9	1.6	3.0	3.0
1997	2.0	1.6	2.9	2.7
1998	2.0	1.5	2.8	2.7
1999	2.0	1.5	2.7	2.5
2000	1.9	1.5	2.7	2.4
2001	2.0	1.5	2.5	2.5
2002	2.1	1.5	2.5	2.4
2003	1.9	1.4	2.6	2.4
2004	2.0	1.4	2.6	2.2
2005	1.9	1.4	2.5	2.5
2006	1.8	1.3	2.5	2.4
2007	1.4	1.3	2.4	2.5
2008	1.3	1.3	2.3	2.2

Source: NATO (http://www.nato.int/cps/en/natolive/topics_49198.htm?selectedLocale=en)

The decrease in military spending does not imply an isolationist attitude; rather, it has occurred concomitantly with increased involvement in international crises (see figures 5.11 and 5.12). As a result, what we are witnessing is not a retreat but rather an increase in activism, with tools other than the military being employed.

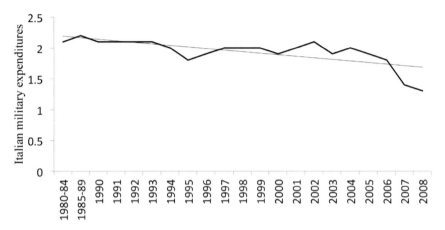

Figure 5.11. Italy's military expenditure as a percentage of GDP. Source: NATO (http://www.nato.int)

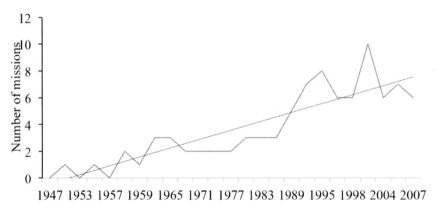

Figure 5.12. Italy's participation in U.N. missions. Source: Attinà (2009: 153)

This negative trend in military expenditures, even as international exposure was increasing, belies neorealist hypotheses, which would have predicted increased spending, either for defensive purposes (to compensate for the weakening of alliances) or for offensive motives (to take advantage of the opportunities for assertion that opened up with the end of the bipolarism).

In terms of organization, the sudden end of the Cold War opened to the Italian armed forces an unexpected window of opportunity.[5] They were transformed from being a conscript army that spent most of its time in barracks and was trained to operate in traditional conflicts to a professional army capable of rapidly intervening in crisis areas and operating in peacekeeping and peace-enforcing missions. An attempt to increase the investment quota of defense spending accompanied these developments. Since the 9/11 attacks, spending on the modernization of weapons systems has been increasing, although it slowed down in 2005 and 2006 due to economic difficulties.

In 2007 and 2008, the modernization program took off again, with more new money being invested in hardware than in personnel, although the latter still comprised the largest item in the defense budget (table 5.2). These efforts, although limited, were aimed at creating a more modern army whose focus is on technology rather than on manpower, as was also the case in other countries. The structure of military spending (e.g. aircraft carriers, tactical transport helicopters, and new-generation fighter jets), and the move from a conscript to a professional army reveal a certain tendency to give Italy a greater capacity for force-projection.

Table 5.2 Distribution of Defense Function funds (millions of euros)

Sector	2007	2008	Difference	Difference (%)
Personnel	8819,9	9110,1	290,2	3,3
Operation	2356,9	2663,2	306,4	13,0
Investment	3272,0	3635,0	362,9	11,1
Total	14.448,8	15.408,3	959,5	6,6

Source: Accompanying note to the Defense Budget

Changes in military policy have occurred within the parameters determined by the strategic culture, sometimes pushing these parameters to their limits, but never breaking them. Military expenditure has been remodulated according to an approach that continues to give priority to accommodationist policies and considers only as a last resort the use of force, especially when offensive. Policy-makers, the elite, and public opinion all continue to favor a multidimensional and integrated approach, which uses soft power whenever possible.[6] The use of force is considered a tool to be employed only in extreme cases, in a limited manner, and under stringent political and military restrictions. Italy's increased force-projection capacity has thus far been used solely for peacekeeping or peace-enforcing missions. Italy is also continuing to seek multilateral cover (U.N., NATO, EU, OSCE) whenever it is involved in operations that imply recourse to the use of force. The most radical innovations were "domesticated" by the national strategic culture. In moments of change, culture affects behavior both by prescribing the repertoire of practicable actions, and by competing with other cultural models and providing the guidelines for conceiving new strategies of action (Swidler 1986).

ITALY AND INTERNATIONAL ORGANIZATIONS

Policy-makers who espouse a nonmilitarized strategic culture are very likely to entrust the resolution of conflicts to multilateral institutions, whereas hard-liners prefer unilateral solutions because they are unwilling to limit their ability to choose whatever strategy they may consider to be most suited to the pursuit of the national interest (Vasquez 1993: ch. 6). Italy has been a strong supporter of multilateral security organizations. A document by the Ministry of Foreign Affairs regarding Italy's participation in international organizations stated that (MAE 2009: 7):

> [. . .] multilateralism, centered on the role of the U.N. (the most legitimate source of authority in the world today), has always been a foreign policy priority for Italy. The spread of conditions of international peace and security, political stability and economic growth, the safeguarding of human dignity and rights, the fight against terrorism and the proliferation of weapons of mass destruction all require effective and efficient cooperation between States in their various multilateral theatres. This approach has led Italy to take on increasing national responsibilities in order to help solve the main issues in European and international politics, ranging from the Middle East to the Balkans, and to Afghanistan. With its participation in a large number of peacekeeping missions, that in 2008 involved the use of about 9,000 troops deployed in the various crisis theatres, Italy has become a country that "produces" security and stability. Italy's actions assign great importance to the humanitarian component and to the solution—shared by the countries involved each time—of the problems addressed that often stem from underdevelopment and lack of dialogue between cultures and religions.

As Fulvio Attinà wrote in a work on multilateralism (2009: 98): "there are factors which favor Italy's perseverance in its multilateralist role, like the fact that this role has been internalized in the country's prevalent political culture, and the experience it has gained through its frequent involvement in multilateral organizations, especially in the European organizations."[7] Throughout the Cold War, Italy strongly supported large international organizations such as the U.N, NATO, and the European community. Its principal interventions in crisis areas have always been under the auspices of these organizations. And this stance has been strengthened, not weakened, since the Berlin Wall came down.

Italy's participation in multilateral missions began in the late 1950s, when—shortly after being admitted into the U.N.—the country took part in various peacekeeping missions in the planet's hot areas:[8]

- Middle East, in 1958 (UNTSO and UNOGIL).
- Southern Asia (UNMOGIP in 1961 and UNIPOM in 1965).
- Congo, in 1960–1962 (ONUC).
- Yemen, in 1964–1965 (UNYOM).

The mission in Congo turned out to be the most complex and dramatic for Italy, resulting in the loss of twenty-one Italian soldiers. A breakthrough in its participation in multilateral missions occurred in the mid-1980s with the first mission in Lebanon (UNIFIL I) that involved the deployment of a large contingent.

The end of the Cold War and of the military blocs logic did not generate a weakening of the support to the multilateral organizations. The legitimation provided by multilateral institutions is considered essential, by public opinion and political class alike, for the country's participation in missions that envisage the use of the military instrument. The data resulting from various studies (Attinà 2009; Foradori, Rosa 2010) show that Italy has participated in approximately one third of all peacekeeping missions conducted by the United Nations (table 5.3). The number of missions, as well as the size of the troops involved, rose after 1988.

Table 5.3 Italy's participation in U.N.'s missions

Name	Location	Italian troops assigned
MINURSO (Referendum in Western Sahara)	Morocco	5
UNFICYP (UN Peacekeeping Force in Cyprus)	Cyprus	4
UNMOGIP (UN Military Observer Group)	India-Pakistan	7
UNAMID	Sudan	28
UNFIL	Lebanon	2,470
MFO (Multinational Force and Observers)	Egypt	78
UNTSO	Israel	7
Total Italian contribution to U.N. operations		*2,599*

Source: Ministry of Defense (http://www.difesa.it/Operazioni+Militari/missioni_attività _internazionali)

In addition to the missions under the aegis of the U.N., Italy has also participated in missions with European multilateral organizations (table 5.4). More specifically, Italy has participated in all nine missions headed by NATO, including some quite onerous in terms of human and material resources deployed as well as being quite risky. Italy's activism has grown with regard to other European organizations, too. This acceleration is the result of the greater role played by the EU in the field of security following the creation of the CFSP/ESDP. Italy has also participated in various missions supported by the OSCE.

Table 5.4 Missions conducted under the aegis of European multilateral organizations

NATO Missions

Name	Location	Italian troops assigned
IFOR	Balkans	2,000
SFOR	Balkans	2,000
XFOR	Balkans	1,000
KFOR	Balkans	2,200
TFH	Balkans	1,000
TFF	Balkans	100
OAH	Balkans	42
ISAF	Afghanistan	1,950
NTM-I	Iraq	44
Total Italian troops		*10,336*

CFSP missions

Name	Location	Italian troops assigned
CONCORDIA	Macedonia	27
EUFOR ALTHEA	Bosnia-Herzegovina	882
EUFOR DR Congo	Congo	56
EUSEC	Congo	4
(EU support to) AMIS	Sudan	6
EUFOR TCHAD/RCA	Chad	105
EU NAVAR	Somalia	225
Total Italian troops		*1,305*

OSCE missions

Name	Location	Italian troops assigned
Spillover Monitor Mission to Skopje	Macedonia	7
LTM Moldova	Moldavia	1
LTM to Bosnia and Herzegovina	Bosnia-Herzegovina	12

Table 5.4 (continued)

LTM to Croatia	Croatia	4
LTM in Kosovo	Kosovo	20
LTM to Serbia	Serbia	5
LTM to Montenegro	Montenegro	1
Total Italian troops		*50*

Source: ADISM DATASET (http://www.fscpo.unict.it/adism/dataitaly.pdf), and Ministry of Defense (http://www.difesa.it/Operazioni+Militari/missioni_attività_internazionali)

Post–Cold War data show that Italy's involvement in multilateral peacekeeping missions has continued to increase, and this commitment has been acknowledged by the other States via the assignment to Italy of leading command and responsibility roles in the management of operations. Therefore, "the analysis of the data confirms the statements of those who sustain that Italy is truly committed to playing the role of multilateralist country in the international security theatre" (Attinà 2009: 97).

MILITARY OPERATIONS (1990–2008)

In order to avoid the risk of engaging in tautological reasoning (i.e., to infer the existence of a culture from the type of behavior observed), in this paragraph I shall not take into consideration the cases presented in chapter 4 to illustrate the characteristics of Italy's strategic culture. Instead I shall focus on Italy's international behavior in the post–Cold War period. I shall analyze the debates held on the occasion of the main international interventions implying the use of force so as to highlight the motivations given. It is a fact that public motivations may not coincide with real ones. Political speeches, the narrations created to illustrate a decision, however, are an important indicator of the actions considered acceptable within a given strategic culture.[9] Narration is not only a rhetorical cover-up but also has practical effects.

In the post–Cold War period (1990–2008), Italy took part in eight major military operations.[10] During some of these, Italian soldiers found themselves under heavy fire:

- The first Gulf War (1991)
- Mozambique (1992)
- Somalia (1993)
- Bosnia (1995)

- Kosovo (1999)
- Afghanistan (2001)
- The second Gulf War (2003)
- Lebanon (2006)

The first crisis of the post–Cold War period occurred on August 2, 1990, when Kuwait was invaded by Saddam Hussein's Iraq. On August 6, the U.N. Security Council voted for the commercial, financial, and military embargo of Iraq. On August 25, with thirteen votes in favor and the abstention of Cuba and Yemen, it authorized the use of force to impose compliance with the embargo. In September, the embargo was extended to the airspace. Finally, on November 29, the decision was taken to authorize the use of force should Iraq fail to withdraw its troops from Kuwait by January 15, 1991. Iraq did not comply with this request and war broke out on the night between January 16 and 17.

The worsening of the situation and the prospect of intervention by the American ally placed Italy facing a dilemma regarding whether or not to join—for the first time since World War II—a war operation. At the beginning of the crisis, when it still wasn't clear which direction the events would take, the Italian government, headed by the Premier Giulio Andreotti (Christian Democrat), with Gianni De Michelis (Italian Socialist Party) then minister of foreign affairs and Virginio Rognoni (Christian Democrat) minister of defense, illustrated Italy's official position (IAI 1993: 111):

> The Council of Ministers once again confirms the international intolerability of the military occupation of Kuwait and of its alleged dismissal as a sovereign State; it appreciates the prompt and unanimous condemnation voted by the U.N. Security Council; it declares its full availability for other U.N. initiatives in addition to those that Italy has already implemented via specific legislative decrees. Italy's availability is once again confirmed as regards every possible defensive support required by the countries of the area that feel threatened; it appreciates the timely stances taken by the Atlantic Alliance and by the European political cooperation. In particular, it reconfirms NATO's united commitment to ensuring security in Turkey; it is happy to see the United States' promptness in providing for Saudi Arabia's defensive needs, thus preventing the spread of Iraq's "adventure." In order to allow this intervention, Italy has approved for utmost logistic cooperation [. . .] The Council of Ministers [disapproves] the Iraqi adventure also because it injures the prestige of the Arab population [. . .] and reiterates Italy's commitment, also during its Presidency of the European Community, to do its utmost to fully restore international legality, reinforced by a strong participation in the development of less advanced populations.

This statement set down the political parameters of Italian participation for the entire duration of the crisis. Italy contributed with a fighter-bomber squadron that carried out various missions in the Iraqi skies.

The government's statement and the ensuing political debate both clearly indicate the problems that a nation with a nonmilitarized strategic culture faces when it is called to take part in war operations. From many sides it was stressed that the recourse to force was in contrast with the constitution. During the parliamentary debate, one of the first to question the legitimacy of a military action was a member of the DC, jurist Giuseppe Guarino, who recalled the pacifist nature of the Italian Constitution and the constraints it placed on any involvement in military operations against Iraq.[11] The main groups opposing the war were from the Communist Party (who in fear of splits to the left voted against military intervention although it had abstained when it had come to vote on the embargo), and the Catholic world, championed by the Pope. All this put the Andreotti government in a tight spot (Donovan 1992).

As a result of the political opposition coming from various fronts—including that of the ruling majority, in which the Liberal and Republican parties were more openly in favor of a military intervention[12]—Italy's line of action ended up being fraught with fine distinctions and caveats:

- The operation could take place only with the approval of the U.N.
- It should be consistent with the positions expressed within the European Community.
- Every other possible alternative means would have to be used before turning to the use of arms.
- Italy's participation would take place only in compliance with precise limitations as concerns the tasks envisaged.

An evidence of the resistance to the operation was the fact that the government insisted from the start in defining it as an "international policing operation" and not as an act of war. This was stated for the first time by the defense minister during the parliamentary debate held on August 23, on the occasion of the decision to send a naval squadron in support of the embargo. In his speech, Minister Rognoni stressed that it was not "a war operation but an operation the aim of which was to ensure and guarantee the embargo sanctioned [. . .] by the U.N. Security Council under resolution No. 661 [. . .] the nations that support the U.N. resolutions do not want war but the respect of the right and the restoration of international legality."[13]

The government held on tightly to this line of action even when the attacks on Baghdad began, following the expiry of the January 15 ultimatum and the failure of the Soviet Union's attempt to negotiate (a diplomatic initiative strongly supported by Rome). In his speech to the Chamber of Deputies on January 16, Prime Minister Giulio Andreotti reiterated the government's line of action, declaring that "the vocation of our country does not consist in following individual initiatives but rather in participating with our partners in security missions based on the U.N.'s central role [. . .] it is our duty to vote in favor of the use of force when it is considered as an extreme *measure of international policing* at the service of the U.N.'s resolutions" (italics added).[14] Roberto Aliboni summarizes as follows (1993: 111):

> On this basis, Italy contributed to the international effort dedicated to defending Saudi Arabia and to liberating Kuwait from occupation by Iraq, staying closely within the sphere of action defined by the U.N. Security Council, acting in harmony with the European member states' position and, overall, strictly attributing to its action a defensive and international policing aura.

Much less troubled was Italy's participation in the UNOMOZ mission in Mozambique in 1992, which was one of the U.N.'s classic peacekeeping missions. In the month of October, after years of war and long negotiations, an agreement was signed in Rome between the government forces and the RENAMO rebels. At the beginning of 1993, a multinational contingent of 6,550 troops and observers was sent to Mozambique to implement resolution No. 782 of the Security Council. The mission was under the command of the U.N. Secretary General's special representative, Aldo Ajello from Italy. The mission's main mandates were the supervision of the conflict parties' compliance with the peace agreement, the overseeing of the electoral process, and the surveillance of transport corridors. Rome contributed to UNOMOZ with 1,030 troops, deployed in April 1993 in the Beira Corridor that connects Zimbabwe to the sea. Thanks to its substantial field contribution, the Italian troops were assigned the role of "force of reference" for the other contingencies participating in the mission.[15]

In the same period, Italy found itself mixed up in the Somalia affair, where a humanitarian mission soon transformed into a deadly armed clash between the international forces and the local factions. The international community intervention in Somalia was part of the U.N. UNOSOM mission, and consisted of three phases. The first, UNOSOM I, commenced in April 1992 and lasted until December of the same year, to be replaced with the UNITAF mission, in turn replaced with the UNOSOM II mission in May 1993. The mission's mandate was to protect the humanitarian aids sent to a Somalia faced with famine, and to monitor the ceasefire between the factions at war with each other since the early 1990s.

The end of the Siad Barre dictatorship was followed by a phase of great instability in which various factions, all heavily armed and organized into clans, fought over the control of the land without anyone managing to prevail. On April 24, 1992, the U.N. Security Council voted in favor of resolution No. 751, which established the UNOSOM I mission to monitor the ceasefire between the warring parties and to protect the humanitarian organizations present in Somalia. Resolution No. 794, of December 3, established the UNOSOM II mission—code-named *Restore*

Hope—with the mandate to guarantee minimal security conditions and favor the establishment of a new government.

The U.N.'s decision was in some important ways different from previous peacekeeping missions (Croci 1994: 191):

- It was not based on an explicit request by the country that was the target of operations.
- It was not justified on the basis of humanitarian aid but rather on chapter 7 of the U.N. that authorizes actions in the case of threats to the peace.
- The use of force was envisaged even in cases other than self-defense.

Because Italy was interested in the region due to its colonial past, it decided to join the multinational force.[16] The first divisions arrived in Somalia on December 13. Unfortunately, the situation deteriorated quickly, and what was intended to be a classic peacekeeping mission became a more complex peace-enforcement operation, with the aim of disarming the "warlords." This caused a violent reaction of the local warlords against the contingents already deployed on location: Pakistani contingent lost twenty-three troops during the "Radio" battle (June 5), the American troops and the Italian corps often found themselves in the middle of armed clashes. The most serious episode occurred during the so-called Checkpoint Pasta battle (July 3), when the Italians were ambushed by Somali militiamen, resulting in three Italian soldiers killed and twenty-two injured. The rapid deterioration of the situation following the battle of Mogadishu (October 3), in which many American soldiers were killed, brought to the slow withdrawal of international forces. Italy began its withdrawal on January 16, 1994, and the operation was concluded two months later.

The changed nature of the operations in Somalia that followed the attacks against the foreign troops—to which the United States reacted with heavy bombings that caused many victims among Somali civilians and generated strong resentment against the multinational forces—sparked heated debate in Italy. If until then the Italian parties and the public alike had supported the mission, the sudden development produced tension and criticism. The Italian government especially was concerned that the American obsession with the capture of one of the warlords, General Aidid, would distract from the mission's real objective and prejudice the image of the contingent's neutrality in the eyes of the Somalis. All this degenerated into a serious political and diplomatic clash between Italy and the United Nations regarding how the mission was to be conducted. The most critical point was reached with the U.N.'s request, later withdrawn, to recall the Italian commander, General Bruno Loi.

Behind the confrontation between Italy and the command of the UNOSOM mission there was the fact that Italian policy-makers attributed greater importance to negotiating strategies. The Italian government argued that—with the change of strategy imposed after the battles with the Pakistanis, Italians, and Americans—diplomacy had been sacrificed in favor of a military line. The difference in approach among the American and Italian high commands was summarized in an article by the BBC correspondent in Rome, published in the *New York Times* on July 22, 1993, with the headline "In Somalia, Machiavelli vs. Rambo." The article highlighted Italy's different approach to the peacekeeping missions. "Italy's criticism is based not just on self-interest but on an entirely different conception of the peacekeeping mission. Italian politics is exceptional in its reliance on compromise, so it's hardly surprising that Rome places a high priority on negotiation."[17]

Although the mission in Somalia demonstrated the country's increased assertiveness in international politics after the end of the logic of the blocs, it is also true that the manner in which this activism was implemented is symptomatic of a nonmilitarized strategic culture that places diplomacy at the top of the list of international strategies.

The war in former Yugoslavia forced Italy to engage in a new military mission in a high-risk area. The crisis began with Slovenia's declaration of independence on June 25, 1991, followed by that of Croatia in September and of Bosnia in 1992. These events triggered bloody conflict in the period from 1991 to 1995 between the secessionist republics, the Serbs who lived in these areas and wished to remain loyal to the central government, and the authorities of Belgrade that were opposed to the dissolution of the federation and supported the groups of Serbian ethnicity. The war ended in the fall of 1995 with the accords of Dayton, Ohio, signed between November 1 and 26 by the representatives of all the warring parties.

The Italian action in Bosnia shows signs of the country's traditional foreign policy—low profile, tendency to move in a multilateral frame—as well as elements of greater military assertiveness. It gave rise to a series of missions:

- Humanitarian assistance conducted under the aegis of the Western European Union Organization (WEU) (1992). Due to the disastrous conditions generated by the onset of the conflict, the European member states decided to send aids to the civilians. Italy took part in military missions to ensure delivery and distribution of the aids. These operations caused very little domestic debate, until the shooting down of a helicopter caused the death of three Italian nationals.
- Participation in the naval blockade, authorized by NATO and by WEU, in order to impose the arms embargo against Serbia (1992).
- Logistic support to the air operations conducted by NATO during the *Deny Flight* operation (1993). Italy supported its allies by mak-

ing available its air bases. At first, only reconnaissance missions flew out from these air bases, but following U.N. resolution No. 958, bombing missions against Serbian positions also began to depart from them.
- Participation in bombing missions in Bosnia (1995). In September, Italy began providing a more active type of support to allied air missions, taking part directly in several air to ground attack operations.
- Sending of troops in support of the IFOR mission organized to enforce the Dayton Accords (1995). Italy sent a contingent of 2,549 troops. The mission was approved by all political parties with the exception of the extreme left parties.

During the crisis, many voices were lifted from the opposition and from the majority parties alike, invoking greater commitment on the field. One of the events that precipitated a heated public debate about the opportunity of sending Italian troops was the statement released by President of the Republic Oscar Luigi Scalfaro on July 15, 1995:

> What is happening against the Muslim enclaves is a show of such a tragic nature, of such human misery, of such suffering that it cannot but generate great rebellion [. . .] faced with this terrible problem of bloodshed, tragedy, and criminality in former Yugoslavia, one must not speak solely of war—which is already per se inhuman and antihuman—[. . .] here we are talking about the criminal who takes innocent people away and threatens to kill them if the police forces try to capture him. It is impossible to just wait and see.[18]

The words of the president were met with approval by both the right-wing and left-wing parties. Even the public opinion was for an interventionist position (Bellucci 1997: 253 and ff.). Despite all this—as further evidence of Italy's unease in taking part in missions that imply the massive use of force—the policy-makers moved very cautiously and, only after the Dayton Accords, decided to join the ground mission, that was justified as a traditional peacekeeping operation. As some analysts put it, the policy-makers' caution was mostly dictated by:

> [. . .] political cultures, rooted in the Catholic and Communist traditions, that did not always welcome high profile foreign policy. No concept of "civil power" was applied to Italy to describe Italian new status in the post–Cold War era, abundantly used instead to describe Germany, even if Italy followed the same strategy of its German counterpart when involved in international issues, such as multilateral approach to international crises and the use of force legitimized by the approval of the international community. It was the very concept of "power" that was contrary to the principles of the Italian political culture. Italy showed much insecurity when it was called to solve strategic and mili-

tary dilemmas, even if they involved the promotion of peace in situations of crisis (Pirani 2004: 41).

A resurgence of the Balkan wars occurred in 1999 with the crisis in Kosovo, a Serbian province with a Muslim majority. On September 23, 1998, the U.N. Security Council voted a resolution (No. 1199) in which it condemned the violent security operations conducted by Serbia forces against Kosovo civilians, demanding an immediate ceasefire and defining the situation as a risk for the region's security and peace.[19] Faced with Belgrade's resistance, NATO launched an ultimatum on October 13, threatening to start a bombing campaign should the hostilities not cease and Serbia should not comply with the resolution. Due to the worsening of the situation, the Contact Group, formed by the U.S., Russia, France, Germany, the UK, and Italy, invited the warring parties to negotiate and reach a diplomatic solution. The negotiations took place in Rambouillet in the months of February and March, but they failed due to Serbia's refusal to accept the draconian conditions imposed. As a consequence, military operations started with the bombing of Serbian targets. This in turn caused the Serbs to retaliate against the Kosovo populations, thus worsening the humanitarian conditions of the civilians.

On March 26, during the parliamentary debate, Italian Prime Minister Massimo D'Alema declared that Italy's involvement would be restrained and that the country would undertake to back the resumption of the negotiations and the end of the bombings. In order to hold together the various "souls" of the government, dominated by pacifist positions contrary to the intervention, this was presented as a necessity dictated by the obligation of loyalty to NATO and to alleviate the dramatic humanitarian crisis (Croci 2000: 120). To stress the humanitarian aspect of the operation, in the first days of April the Arcobaleno mission was launched to assist the refugees who had sought shelter in Albania. On April 13, D'Alema reiterated the main points of the government's action:

> I want to insist here on the fact that our support to NATO derives from an in-depth reflection that has preceded and accompanied this commitment, and especially from a rigorous analysis, including moral argumentations, on the legitimate use of force. This reflection is all the more delicate in a country such as ours, where the deep feelings of aversion for violence and of sincere and consolidated friendship for other populations—especially for those closer to us on the other side of the Adriatic Sea—made it rather difficult to decide in favor of military action [. . .] I believe that the majority of Italian citizens have understood our decisions and our acceptance of responsibility. They have understood that the use of force is an extreme solution, albeit inevitable when faced with a tragedy that cannot be contained otherwise. Regarding this aspect, even the U.N. Secretary General, Kofi Annan, specifically stated in his speech in Geneva a few days ago that (I quote): "It is emerging slowly, but I believe surely, an international norm against the violent

repression of minorities, a norm that will and must take precedence over concerns of State sovereignty." It is obvious that, due to its implications, this principle requires utmost political prudence, a wide source of legitimization, and definite codification in terms of international law.[20]

The speech underlined several recurrent themes of Italian foreign policy: reference to the international legitimacy ensured by the multilateral organizations; the use of weapons only as last resort; the emergence of international law for the protection of human rights; and the traditional aversion for the use of force.

In the course of events, the Italian forces participated in warfare operations. The prime minister declared that these operations were all part of the "integrated defense mission of the territory," that was the formula adopted after the conflict to describe the nature of Italy's military participation. In addition to military actions, the Italian authorities worked constantly to favor the search for a negotiated solution and the suspension of war operations.[21] On May 6, the foreign ministers of the G8 countries drafted a peace plan that envisaged the ceasefire, the withdrawal of all military and paramilitary forces from Kosovo, the deployment of an international contingent to supervise compliance with the agreement, the return of the refugees, a widespread autonomy for the region, and measures for favoring its development. After almost another month of heavy bombing, Belgrade declared it was ready to accept the G8 peace plan. With the end of hostilities, the KFOR mission was launched in Kosovo, on June 12, which also included an Italian contingent that by the end of 1999 totaled almost six thousand men.

According to the analysts, Italy's participation in the conflict was rather tempered. "Italy's main contribution to the military mission in Yugoslavia consisted in logistics, while its participation in air force sorties was limited. Its major contribution consisted of its support to the stabilization forces entering Kosovo" (Gasparini 2000: 163–64). When it came to the more controversial operations, such as ground bombing, the Italian military action was affected not only by the technical limitations of the means employed, but also by the "political issues connected to this allegedly 'aggressive' use of air force" (Ibid.: 160). Moreover, throughout the crisis, the "Italian government never [renounced] its traditional penchant for keeping open a channel of dialogue with Belgrade, for constantly seeking cooperation with Russia, and for reconfirming the role of the U.N. in managing international crises" (Greco 2000: 137).

In the aftermath of the 9/11 terrorist attacks on the United States, Italy found itself involved in what turned out to be most probably the two most complex military operations of the post–World War II period, that is, those in Afghanistan (2001) and in Iraq (2003). In order to punish the countries suspected of helping the terrorists, in the autumn of 2001 the

Bush administration launched a military operation against Afghanistan that was governed by the Talibans. The conflict began on November 7, following the failure of negotiations to secure custody of Osama Bin Laden and of other members of the Al-Qaeda organization. U.S. troops were immediately flanked by British troops. The Taliban forces, caught between the U.S. air attacks and the offensive operations of the Northern Alliance, were soon forced to abandon Kabul. The end of November saw the opening of an international conference in Petersberg, in the environs of Bonn, to discuss the future political assets of the country where, however, the clashes were still ongoing and the resistance of the Talibans in their strongholds did not look easily breakable at all.

Faced with the escalation of these events, the position of the Berlusconi government was to readily support the American intervention. On October 9, the Italian Parliament approved a motion to support the United States in the fight against international terrorism and the war in Afghanistan. One month later (November 7), the Chambers approved Italy's participation in the mission called *Enduring Freedom*. On December 20, the U.N. Security Council authorized the creation of a multinational force (ISAF), with the task of protecting and helping the new government in Kabul. In August 2003, the command of ISAF was handed over to NATO. Italy took part in the mission by sending various thousands of troops, deployed in the Kabul and Herat areas.[22]

The political debate regarding Italy's intervention was focused on two key issues: the role of international legitimization and the problem of the caveats and of the rules of engagement (the political and military restrictions placed on the soldiers' action). In the speech held before the Chamber of Deputies on November 7, these two problems were underlined by the then Defense Minister Antonio Martino:

> The first communications of the government after the terrorist attacks were made on September 13 to the Defense and Foreign Affairs Commissions of the Chamber of Deputies and of the Senate in a joint session. On that occasion, the Parliament was informed, among other things, about the statement of the Atlantic Council that classified the attacks in the United States as events capable of triggering the mechanisms of Article 5 of the Washington Treaty. It is worth recalling here that Article 5 states that an armed attack against one or more allied countries in Europe or in North America shall be considered an armed attack against all members of the Alliance and, consequently, that each member of the Alliance, in exercise of the right of individual or collective self-defense recognized by Article 51 of the Charter of the United Nations, will assist the ally or allies so attacked by taking, individually and in concert with the other parties, such action as it deems necessary, including the use of armed force [. . .] The forces engaged in Operation Enduring Freedom belong to various nationalities. Necessarily, they must have the same rules of engagement so as to ensure uniformity in behavior and intent. To date, the American Command directing opera-

tions has not provided any indications regarding this topic. As soon as the rules of engagement are made known for this operation, they shall be analyzed in order to establish their applicability by the Italian troops, both in terms of operativeness and of legality.[23]

Faced with the perplexities of the political opposition regarding the compatibility of the rules of engagement with Italian laws, the minister argued that "obviously, should the rules not fully comply with the mission or with the law, they shall not be accepted."[24]

Due to these political difficulties, the Italian contingent was hindered by a series of caveats that severely limited its operations and its capacity to conduct offensive actions. The first limitation concerned the time required to respond to allies' requests, quite prudentially set at seventy-two hours. The second concerned the rules of engagement that defined the situations in which the troops were allowed to attack enemy forces. While several countries participating in the ISAF mission also used preventive actions against the Talibans, the Italian contingent, along with the German and Spanish ones, envisaged the use of force only in response to an attack. These limitations led to ample agreement on the mission, also among the main opposition parties. Subsequently, in 2008, the Berlusconi government partially lifted the limitations placed on the Italian contingent.

In May 2003, the operation called Ancient Babylon was launched, following the Second Gulf War that was officially ended in May, with President Bush declaring the end of major combat operations from the deck of the aircraft carrier USS Abraham Lincoln. With the beginning of the post-conflict phase, on May 22, the U.N. Security Council issued resolution No. 1483 that invited the international community to join in Iraq's reconstruction effort and in the creation of basic stability and security conditions.

The Italian troops were deployed in the country's southern region with a Shiite majority, relatively more peaceful compared to the rest of Iraq. The general headquarters of the Italian contingent was located in the city of Nasiriyah, and this is where, on November 12, the worst attack occurred, killing twelve Carabinieri, five soldiers, and two civilians. On April 6, 2004 the Italian troops were engaged in a violent armed clash with the Mahdi army that lasted five hours and left eleven Italian soldiers injured and approximately fifteen Iraqi troops dead. The mission was ended on December 1, 2006 by the Prodi government.

Operation Ancient Babylon had been approved by the Italian Parliament in April 2003, when combat was still underway. In his speech to the Senate, Minister of Foreign Affairs Franco Frattini illustrated the position of the Italian government as follows:

> Italy will strive for the adoption at international level of an organic plan for the reconstruction of Iraq. It considers urgent to prepare an

operation addressing the humanitarian emergency that is affecting the Iraqi population, and that is on the verge of becoming an even worse catastrophe than the war itself. To this end, the inter-ministerial task force has prepared a project for sustaining and aiding the Iraqi population that is based on the sectors in which the experience and expertise gained by Italy in humanitarian cooperation and in peacekeeping missions are universally acknowledged [. . .] The dire public order conditions in Iraq, the difficulties met in distributing aids, the risks of plunder and of speculation, however, demand the implementation of adequate measures of military coverage so as to guarantee the basic security conditions necessary for achieving the objectives of the Italian humanitarian activities. Thus, a contingent of about 3,000 units shall protect the flow of aids, shall open the communication avenues and airport infrastructures, shall defuse bombs and floating mines, shall supervise the detection of any biological or chemical agents, and shall help in keeping the public order during aid operations.[25]

Similarly to what had happened on the occasion of the First Gulf War, the mission was not presented as a military action but as a humanitarian operation that, due to local instability, required the presence of soldiers.

The soft approach to the post-conflict situation in Iraq, on the one hand, proved successful, and the Italian troops managed to "appear more as security forces rather than an occupation army and therefore managed to develop positive relationships with the local authorities and with the newly formed local police" (Aliboni, Bonvicini 2005: 104). On the other hand, the fact of considering the mission as a contribution to the reconstruction and pacification of the country and not as an action in a war theatre, conditioned the composition of the contingent, the choice of means and, last but not least, the "soft" defense system adopted at the Maestrale base in Nasiriyah, which was considered inadequate during an internal investigation of the army. The only way to defend the base would have been to close all access routes, and the deployment of heavy weapon systems, but this was in contrast with the humanitarian nature of the mission that required interaction with the locals.[26]

The UNIFIL II mission was launched in Lebanon in 2006. The mission stemmed from the crisis that had escalated between Israel and Lebanon in the summer of 2006 when, in response to incursions by Hezbollah militants into Israeli territories and the launching of missiles, the Tel Aviv army had set off a massive military operation. The strong resistance put up by the Hezbollah gave rise to an impasse. A peace conference was summoned in Rome in July, under the aegis of the United States and of Italy and with the participation of Lebanese Prime Minister Siniora and of the Secretary General of the United Nations. The initiative was followed in August by the unanimous approval of resolution No. 1701 of the U.N. Security Council, followed by the Israeli ceasefire and the organization of an international peace force that was meant to guarantee a safety line to keep the opponents separate. The majority of the international contingent, consisting of about fifteen thousand men, was represented by Italy with over twenty-five-hundred troops.

The Lebanon mission did not trigger many political controversies,[27] since it took on the classic guise of a peacekeeping mission aimed to help the two parties comply with the ceasefire. Some dissention arose with regard to the interpretation of the U.N. mandate that remained ambiguous regarding the objective of disarming the Hezbollah militias.

Summing up the features of the various cases analyzed in this section, Italy's international behavior since 1990 reveal the strong influence of its nonmilitarized strategic culture:

- A preference for diplomacy over coercion.
- A preference for wide-spectrum strategies, in which military action acts as a secondary instrument.
- A quest for the international legitimization of interventions, whether it comes from the United Nations, NATO, or other security organizations.
- Multilateralism, by virtue of which Italy never acts alone in a crisis area even when its international interests are directly at stake.
- The framing of interventions as humanitarian operations, peace missions, or international policing activities.
- A rejection of offensive action.
- Strict political and operational constraints on the use of military force in theatres of operation.

The hot political debates triggered by every intervention and the various political and military "strings" attached to their implementation testify to the dilemmas that a country with an accommodationist strategic culture has to face when it is confronted with the need to go to war.

NOTES

1. The statistics regarding Italy's behavior in militarized disputes are the result of the author's original elaboration of aggregate data collected by the project *Correlates of War*. The coding of version 3.0 of the data on MIDs is based the records from version 2.0 and is available online: Jones, Bremer, Singer (1996) (http://www.correlatesofwar.org).

2. In analyzing Italy's military behavior, I have followed an approach similar to that used by Johnston to analyze China's conflictual behavior (1998b).

3. "The success of this model is due most probably to the fact that it has brought on the reconciliation between the Armed Forces and an important majority of the public opinion that, for a long time, had always shown detachment from (when not downright hostility towards) military institutions. The participation in peacekeeping missions has given the military increasing legitimation of their role and activity in the Italian society, and for the political parties it has constituted a point of equilibrium between a more 'traditional' formulation of the defense policy, on the one side, and

the humanitarian and anti-militarist traditions of the catholic world and of the left-wing parties, on the other" (Nuti 2006: 503).

4. The calculation of the Italian military expenditure is a rather complex affair, considering that the defense budget items include expenses that are not closely linked to the defense functions. This means that, in general, the amounts notified by the Defense Ministry are much smaller than those calculated by international organizations like SIPRI or NATO. The latter, in addition to using different criteria to calculate Italy's military expenses, also include expenses, such as the financing of international missions, which are not accounted for in the Italian defense budget. With a view to making the comparison with other countries easier, the NATO data—that are fairly similar to those of SIPRI—has been used. With regard to the problems relating to the defense policy and military expenditure in Italy, see De Andreis, Miggiano (1987), Mayer (1989), Santoro (1992).

5. Part of this section has been taken from Foradori, Rosa (2010).

6. Regarding this point, see Foradori, Rosa (2007a; 2007b).

7. With regard to the socialization processes deriving from the participation in multilateral institutions, see Johnston (2008).

8. This brief historical reconstruction is based on Attinà (2009: ch. 3).

9. With regard to the use of strategic culture as a tool for legitimizing action via the fixation of the coordinates of the official language and of the limitation of the repertoire of available options, see Johnston (1995b).

10. Here I have used the definition of military intervention by Sullivan and Koch (2009: 709): "[The] use of armed force that involves the official deployment of at least 500 regular troops (ground, air, or naval) to attain immediate-term political objectives through actions against a foreign adversary." The political objectives contemplated are: interventions in order to maintain a foreign regime; removing a foreign regime; causing a change in policy; taking or defending a territory; maintaining an empire; supplying social protection and order (peacekeeping missions).

11. *Atti parlamentari, Camera dei deputati, X legislatura, discussioni*, August 23, 1990, pp. 68838–39 (http://legislature.camera.it/_dati/leg10/lavori/stenografici/sed0514/sed0514.pdf).

12. Italy's political actors most affected by the *realpolitik* attitude were those linked to minor parties such as PRI (Italian Republican Party) and PLI (Italian Liberal Party), heirs of the traditions of the Italian *Risorgimento*, as well as to the post-Fascist nationalism.

13. *Atti parlamentari, Camera dei deputati, X legislatura, discussioni*, August 23, 1990, p. 68807 (legislature.camera.it/_dati/leg10/lavori/stenografici/sed0514/sed0514.pdf).

14. *Atti parlamentari, Camera dei deputati, X legislatura, discussioni*, January 16, 1991, p. 77923 (legislature.camera.it/_dati/leg10/lavori/stenografici/sed0574/sed0574.pdf).

15. Italian Defense Ministry (www.esercito.difesa.it/root/attivita/mix_albatros.asp).

16. As Osvaldo Croci points out, in addition to the interest in the former colony there was the traditional "presentialist" policy and the awareness that, with the end of the Cold War, the country had to take on a more decisive role in the supply of international security. "The greatest pressure to convince the government to participate in the mission actually came from top officials of the Ministries of Defense and of Foreign Affairs, who saw in the mission in Somalia the first chance Italy had to play this new role" (Croci 1994: 193).

17. The article is available online on the *New York Times* website (http://www.nytimes.com/1993/07/22/opinion/in-somalia-machiavelli-vs-rambo.html?scp=1&sq=machiavelli%20vs%20rambo&st=cse).

18. *Corriere della sera*, July 15, 1995 (http://archiviostorico.corriere.it/1995/luglio/15/Scalfaro_crimini_ Hitler_Stalin_non _co_0_950715811.shtm).

19. The reconstruction of the Kosovo crisis is based on the conflict's chronology found in Aliboni, Bruni, Colombo, Greco (2000).

20. *Comunicazioni del Governo sugli sviluppi della crisi nei Balcani*, shorthand-written minutes of the Meeting, session No. 518, held on April 13, 1999 (http://www.camera.it/_dati/leg13/lavori/stenografici/sed518/ s250.htm#titolo3496).

21. Italy had shown a clear preference for a diplomatic strategy in the days that preceded the onset of the hostilities. It was rather concerned about the U.S.'s military approach that seemed to drive towards a military clash. The Italian Embassy in Belgrade remained opened throughout the war (Greco 2000).

22. The objective of the Italian mission was to "conduct military operations in Afghanistan consistent with the mandate received, in cooperation and coordinated with the Afghan security forces and in coordination with the coalition forces, so as to assist the Afghan government in maintaining security, to favor the development of government structures, to extend the government's control over the entire country, and to assist the humanitarian efforts and the reconstruction operations through the implementation of the Bonn agreements and of other important international agreements." Ministry of Defense (www.difesa.it/Operazioni+Militari/Operazioni+internazionali+in+corso/Afghanistan+-+ISAF+HQ+-+ITALFOR+KABUL/scheda.htm).

23. *Comunicazioni del Governo sull'impiego di contingenti militari italiani all'estero in relazione alla crisi internazionale in atto*, session No. 57 held on November 7, 2001, shorthand-written minutes of the Meeting, p. 3 (http://legxiv.camera.it/chiosco.asp?sMacrosezione=Docesta&source=&position=Organi%20Parlamentari\L'Assemblea\Resoconti%20dell'Assemblea&content=/_dati/leg14/lavori/stenografici/framedinam.asp?sedpag=sed057/s000r.htm).

24. Ibid., p. 5

25. *Atti parlamentari, Senato, XIV legislatura, resoconto sommario e stenografico*, April 15, 2003, pp. VI-VII (http://www.senato.it/service/PDF/PDFServer?tipo=BGT&id=114257).

26. One of the officers investigated with regard to the Nasiriyah disaster defended his position by stating he had asked Rome for reinforcement of the measures protecting the headquarters, but that his request had gone unacknowledged. This fact would confirm "the difficulty of implementing a peacekeeping mission that actually is conducted in a war zone or a guerrilla zone" (*Corriere della sera*, 13-3-2009. http://www.corriere.it/cronache/09_marzo_13/processo_strage_nassiriya_1e2d3f9a-0f9b-11de948b0014 4f02 aabc.shtml).

27. Rifondazione Comunista, a member of the Prodi government, also supported the mission.

SIX

Conclusions

This book had a dual objective: to describe the sociological turn in international relations and to use the approaches deriving from it to analyze the Italian case. The introduction emphasized how the explanations of a country's behavior underlining the role of anarchy, the position in the international system, and the distribution of power and resources, prove to be imprecise in many cases. Pressure exerted from the outside on foreign policy choices is not stringent enough to provide univocal interpretations of the lines adopted by policy-makers.

This point has recently been acknowledged even by scholars with a realist background, who have renounced the elegance and parsimony of neorealism (or structural realism) schemes to propose a return to the past complexity of traditional realism, in which the variables taken into consideration to explain foreign policy were referred both to the international collocation of a country and to the internal characteristics of the State and of society. Neoclassic realism (Lobell, Ripsman, Taliaferro 2009) proposes to recover the role of intervening variable played by the State-society relationship to explain how a country responds to a particular international event. According to these authors, there is no direct link between what happens on the outside and the way States decide to set up their foreign policy, since national response is conditioned/filtered by a series of domestic variables: the degree of centralization of the decision-making process; the force of the societal actors and the capacity of the foreign policy leaders to resist such pressures; the dominating ideology, more or less extremist and suitable for mobilizing the population towards ambitious foreign policy objectives; the degree of compatibility of the objectives of international politics with other objectives, such as economic development or regime stability; the type of national identity, and so forth. These corrective elements have made neoclassic realism harder to manage, but at the same time have made it possible to elaborate more precise explanations and establish interesting collaborations with other approaches attentive to the domestic dimension of foreign policy decisions, from the domestic structure approach to the studies on security cultures.

The interpretations of Italian foreign policy based on domestic politics resulted to be rather imprecise as well, since they are not able to explain the persistence—during all the time periods considered and despite the changes in the national political system—of some traits such as the preference for diplomatic solutions, a tendency towards the nonmilitarization of threats, the reluctance to use force. The way in which internal political dynamics influence decisions in the security field is filtered by the organizational subcultures of those making such decisions.

The main approaches focused on the ideational bases of international politics have been analyzed in chapters 2 and 3. The characteristics of constructivism and the research area deriving from it, i.e., the security cultures, have been summarized. The seminal work of Katzenstein (1996) and his collaborators embraces a number of cases where the cultural variables play an important role: the decisions of the states in the field of conventional weapons proliferation; the grand strategy of a nation; the influence of emerging international rules on the behavior of the States regarding the use of nuclear weapons; the influence of the development of particular national identities on military policy choices, such as the defense expenditure level, the antimilitarism of the elites and public opinion, the role of the armed forces, and the preference for determined intervention strategies. Sociological institutionalism, examined in chapter 2, makes it possible to answer the question: where do the security cultures of a country (the ideas on the behaviors considered to be appropriate in the military field) come from? The study of learning processes emphasizes the historical and cultural bases of the practices followed by policy-makers on the international level.

The studies on strategic cultures, described in chapter 3, derive from the studies on security cultures. Even though there is no univocal definition of the concept of strategic culture, the ones usually proposed refer to the system of ideas possessed by the policy-makers (politicians and military leaders) of a country regarding the legitimacy and effectiveness of the use of force in international relations. In particular, in this book I have adopted Johnston's definition that distinguishes strategic cultures into two parts. The first includes the symbols expressing the ideas of a group regarding the role of war and of force in international politics; the second includes more operational dimensions, related to preferences for particular strategic options (offensive, defensive, nonmilitary).

Johnston's strategic culture concept was used to analyze the case of Italy. Chapter 4 attempts to reconstruct the main aspects of the Italian strategic culture. To this end, a distinction has been made between the period prior to World War II, on the one side, and Republican Italy born out of the disaster of the war and the dissolution of the Fascist regime, on the other. For each of these periods an attempt has been made to reconstruct the policy-makers' image of the war, the way they conceived relations with other states (in conflictual terms or not), their opinion on the legitimacy and effectiveness of the military instrument to pursue foreign policy objectives, and the various strategic preferences.

In the cases of Liberal (1861–1921) and Fascist (1922–1943/45) Italy, the strategic culture displays many aspects of what Johnston calls the *hard realpolitik* model (Johnston 1995b). In both periods, war was considered by the Italian leaders as a normal fact inherent in the characteristics of the relations among nations. In particular, during the Fascist period war rose to a paroxysmal level of exaltation, where it was seen as a kind of test to select the nations destined to make history or be forgotten by it.

During the Liberal and Fascist periods, international politics often took on a zero-sum connotation, whereby it was very difficult to dialogue with the enemy, whose defeat was considered essential for the fulfillment of national objectives: Austria-Hungary and the reconquering of the *irredente* (unredeemed) lands in World War I, and France and England and the search for an empire in World War II are cases in point. These policy-makers manifested a pragmatic attitude towards force, in which the choice to use it was not dictated by a moralistic vision, but by an opportunistic calculation of its utility in a given circumstance.

As regards strategic preferences, the Liberal period features a strategic culture in which the cult of the offensive prevails. This cult, in the eve of World War I, as demonstrated by Snyder (1984), Van Evera (1984) and others, was disseminated throughout all European states. The Italian political and military leaders were not indifferent to this trend; they too were convinced that the war could be won by rapid offensive actions, despite the advantages the defense achieved with the introduction of machine guns. The cult of the offensive was also present in Fascism.

For countries like Italy, Japan, and Germany, the end of World War II represented a moment of total break with the previous strategic culture. As Vasquez says, the fact that these countries experienced a catastrophic defeat, together with the widespread perception that the war they fought was not worth the tremendous costs borne—in terms of money, human lives and material destruction—favored the rise to power of policy-makers promoting a nonmilitarized type of strategic culture.

The Italian strategic culture of the post–World War II period, embraced by the major political forces of the country, from the left-wing to the catholic parties, has characteristics diametrically opposed to those prevailing in the Liberal and Fascist periods: an image of the war no longer considered to be inevitable in international relations, a less negative conception of the enemy, many doubts about the utility of force, and a strong antimilitaristic attitude. In terms of strategic options it is marked by a clear preference for an international strategy based on the use of diplomatic instruments and a total rejection of offensive actions. In this culture, actors influenced by the old *realpolitik* doctrine still survive. In particular, the small liberal parties and political actors supporting Fascist tradition are standard-bearers of this type of strategic culture.

Numerous factors have contributed to the rooting and institutionalization of this culture: the constitutionalization of the pacifist vocation; the discrediting of the armed forces; the downsizing of the defense industry; the "de-fascistization" process, which was often translated into a de-nationalization process; the creation of the myth of the "compassionate Italian soldier," which has contributed to spread the narrative of a country reluctant to use weapons; the domestic politics' polarization that favored low profile choices in the field of security and defense.

Chapter 5 is an attempt to test the theories derived from the neorealist and strategic culture models. The results are a composite picture, in which the influence exerted by the nonmilitarized strategic culture on the country's international choices are quite evident. Both the quantitative analysis of Italy's participation in military disputes and the more detailed reconstruction of the trend of defense expenditures and of the support to multilateralism, back up the hypothesis of the strategic culture model. The reconstruction of the major military interventions in the post–Cold War period also confirms this interpretation.

This does not mean that structural changes stimulated by the end of the bipolar world have not affected the Italian foreign policy. They have, indeed, and even heavily so, as appears in many points of chapter 5. The cultural explanations do not deny the influence of the structural factors emphasized by the neorealists (while the contrary is not true). They limit themselves to emphasizing how the structural factors, in order to be effective, must be interpreted through the cultural lenses that define the repertories of actions considered to be appropriate by a country's policymakers (a position also accepted by neoclassical realism). On the contrary, for the neorealists, cultural factors have at most a residual role serving to explain deviations from rational behavior (Desch 2005).

Therefore, on the one hand, empirical analysis shows Italy's greater assertiveness on the international scenario. The transformation of the armed forces from a "barrack's" army—based on mandatory conscription—to a professional army capable of carrying out rapid interventions abroad, and the transition from a role of *security taker* to one of *security producer* are good examples of this trend. On the other hand, the way this greater activism is implemented and the constraints characterizing the Italian action in the security arena—from the preference assigned to diplomatic action, to seeking a multilateral legitimation on military interventions, to the conditioned use of military instruments—show the decisive weight of a nonmilitarized strategic culture even in the post–Cold War period that is characterized by the end of the blocs confrontation and the recovery of a greater freedom of action.

Bibliography

Adler E. (1992), "The Emergence of Cooperation: National Epistemic Communities and the International Evolution of the Idea of Nuclear Arms Control," *International Organization*, 46(1): 101–45.
Aga Rossi E., Zaslavsky V. (2005), "La cultura politica della sinistra italiana nel secondo dopoguerra," in Petracchi (a cura di) (2005).
Albonetti A. (1998), "Storia segreta della bomba italiana ed europea," *Limes* n. 2: 157–71.
Aliboni R. (1993), "L'Italia, il Golfo e il Mediterraneo," in IAI (1993).
Aliboni R., Bonvicini G. (2005), "La politica estera dell'Italia," in Colombo, Ronzitti (a cura di) (2005).
Aliboni R., Bruni F., Colombo A., Greco E. (a cura di) (2000), *L'Italia e la politica internazionale*, Bologna, il Mulino.
Allison G. T. (1971), *Essence of Decision: Explaining the Cuban Missile Crisis*, Glenview, IL: Scott Foresman and Company.
Arpino M. (1989), "La dottrina d'impiego delle forze aeree e i criteri della difesa aerea," in Jean (a cura di) (1989).
Attinà F. (2009), *La scelta del multilateralismo. L'Italia e le operazioni di pace*, Milano: Giuffrè.
Bagnato B. (2006), "Tra il passato della guerra e il futuro della pace. Interessi economici e timori politici nell'azione italiana verso l'URSS di Kruschev," in Goglia, Moro, Nuti (a cura di) (2006a).
Banfield E. (1967), *The Moral Basis of a Backward Society*, New York: Free Press.
Barié O. (a cura di) (1988), *L'alleanza occidentale*, Bologna: il Mulino.
Barnett M. (2002), "Historical Sociology and Costructivism: an Estranged Past, a Federated Future?" in Hobden, Hobson (eds.) (2002).
Battistelli F. (1980), *Armi: nuovo modello di sviluppo? L'industria militare in Italia*, Torino: Einaudi.
Beasley R., Kaarbo J., Lantis J., Snarr M. (eds.) (2002), *Foreign Policy in Comparative Perspective*, Washington, DC: CQ Press.
Bellucci P. (1997), "L'intervento italiano in Bosnia e la (lenta) ridefinizione della politica di difesa," in D'Alimonte, Nelken (a cura di) (1997).
Benedict R. (2005), *The Chrysanthemum and the Sword: Patterns of Japanese Culture*, New York: Mariner Books.
Berger T. U. (1996), "Norms, Identity and National Security in Germany and Japan," in Katzenstein (ed.) (1996a).
Booth K. (1979), *Strategy and Ethnocentrism*, New York: Holmer & Meier Publishers, Inc.
Booth K. (1990), "The Concept of Strategic Culture Affirmed," in Jacobsen (ed.) (1990).
Bosworth R. J. B., Romano S. (a cura di) (1991), *La politica estera italiana, 1860–1985*, Bologna: il Mulino.
Caligaris L. (a cura di) (1990), *La difesa europea: proposte e sfide*, Milano: Edizioni di Comunità.
Caligaris L., Santoro C. M. (1986), *Obiettivo difesa*, Bologna: il Mulino.
Cassese S. (1998), *Lo stato introvabile*, Milano: Donzelli.
Cavazza F., Graubard S. (a cura di) (1974), *Il caso italiano*, Milano: Garzanti.
Chabod F. (1965), *Storia della politica estera italiana*, Bari: Laterza.

Checkel J. (1998), "The Constructivist Turn in International Relations Theory," *World Politics* 50(2): 324–48.
Colombo A., Ronzitti N. (a cura di) (2005), *L'Italia e la politica internazionale*, Bologna: il Mulino.
Conti G. (2006), "La guerra del fascismo," in Goglia, Moro, Nuti (a cura di) (2006a).
Coralluzzo V. (2000), *La politica estera dell'Italia repubblicana (1946–1992)*, Milano: Franco Angeli.
Cordesman A. H. (1982), "Deterrence in the 1980s: American Strategic Forces and Exended Deterrence," *Adelphi Papers* no. 175.
Croci O. (1994), "L'intervento italiano in Somalia: una nuova politica estera per il dopo 'guerra fredda'?" in Mershon, Pasquino (a cura di) (1994).
Croci O. (2000), "Dovere, umanitarismo e interesse nazionale. L'Italia e l'intervento della NATO in Kosovo," in Gilbert, Pasquino (a cura di) (2000).
D'Alimonte R., Nelken D. (a cura di) (1997), *Politica in Italia*, Bologna: il Mulino.
D'Amore C. (2001), *Governare la difesa*, Milano: Franco Angeli.
De Andreis M., Miggiano P. (1987), *L'Italia e la corsa agli armamenti*, Milano: Franco Angeli.
De Benedetti F. et al. (1971), *Il potere militare in Italia*, Bari: Laterza.
De Cecco M., Pianta M. (a cura di) (1882), *Amministrazione militare e spesa per armamenti in Europa*, Bologna: il Mulino.
De Felice R. (1974), *Mussolini il duce. Gli anni del consenso. 1929–1936*, Torino: Einaudi.
Desch M. (1998), "Culture Clash: Assessing the Importance of Ideas in Security Studies," *International Security* 23(1): 141–70.
Desch M. (2005), "Culture versus Structure in Post–9/11 Security Studies," *Strategic Insights* 4(10) (http://www.ccc.nps.navy.mil/si/2005/Oct/deschOct05.asp).
Deutsch K. W. et al. (1957), *Political Community and the North Atlantic Area*, Princeton, NJ: Princeton University Press.
Di Nolfo E. (1977), "Dieci anni di politica estera italiana," in Ronzitti (a cura di) (1977).
Di Nolfo E. (1979), "Sistema internazionale e sistema politico italiano: interazione e compatibilità", in Graziano, Tarrow (a cura di) (1979).
Di Nolfo E. (2006), "Guerra, Stato e nazione nel secondo dopoguerra," in Goglia, Moro, Nuti (a cura di) (2006a).
Donovan M. (1992), "Il pacifismo cattolico e la guerra del Golfo," in Hellman, Pasquino (a cura di) (1992).
Dottori G., Gasparini G. (2001), "Italy's Changing Defence Policy," *International Spectator* 36(4): 51–59.
Dottori G., Laporta P. (1995), "La definizione e la rappresentanza degli interessi nazionali dell'Italia nel nuovo sistema multi-istituzionale di sicurezza europea," *Rivista Militare* 68: 111–48.
Dougherty J. E., Pfaltzgraff R. L. (1971), *Contending Theories of International Relations*, Philadelphia: Lippicot Company.
Doyle M., Ikenberry G. J. (eds.) (1997), *New Thinking in International Relations Theory*, Boulder, CO: Westview Press.
Duffield J. (1999), "Political Culture and State Behavior: Why Germany Confounds Neorealism," *International Organization* 53(4): 765–803.
Evangelista M. (1995), "Transnational Relations, Domestic Structure, and Security Policy in the USSR and Russia," in Risse-Kappen (ed.) (1995).
Evangelista M. (1997), "Domestic Structure and International Change," in Doyle, Ikenberry (eds.) (1997).
Ferraris L. V. (a cura di) (1996), *Manuale della politica estera italiana*, Bari-Roma: Laterza.
Finnemore M. (1996a), *National Interests in International Society*, Ithaca, NY: Cornell University Press.
Finnemore M. (1996b), "Norms, Culture, and World Politics: Insights from Sociology's Institutionalism," *International Organization* 50(2): 325–47.

Focardi F., Klinkhammer L. (2006), "La rimozione dei crimini di guerra dell'Italia fascista: la nascita di un mito autoassolutorio (1943–1948)," in Goglia, Moro, Nuti (a cura di) (2006a).
Foradori P., Rosa P. Scartezzini R. (2008), *Immagini del mondo. Introduzione alle relazioni Internazionali*, Milano: Vita e Pensiero.
Foradori P., Rosa P. (2007a), "Italy: New Ambitions and Old Deficiencies," in Kirchner, Sperling (eds) (2007).
Foradori P., Rosa P. (2007b), "National Threats Perceptions: Survey Results from Italy," *GARNET Working Paper* 18/7 (http://www.garnet-eu.org/fileadmin/documents/working_papers/1807/5.3.2%20contents.pdf).
Foradori P., Rosa P. (2010), "Italy: Hard Tests and Soft Responses," in Kirchner, Sperling (eds.) (2010).
Forlati Picchio L. (1988), "Rapporti NATO–Nazioni Unite e costituzione italiana: profili giuridici," in Bariè (cura di) (1988).
Formigoni G. (2005), "La cultura internazionale della Democrazia Cristiana," in Petracchi (a cura di) (2005).
Freedman L. (1989), *The Evolution of Nuclear Strategy*, Basingstoke, UK: Macmillan.
Gaja R. (1995), *L'Italia nel mondo bipolare*, Bologna: il Mulino.
Garruccio L. (pseud. di Ludovico Incisa di Camerana) (1982), "Le scelte di fondo e il retroterra culturale," *Politica Internazionale* X: 7–14.
Gasparini G. (2000), "La partecipazione all'intervento militare," in Aliboni, Bruni, Colombo, Greco (a cura di) (2000).
Cavazza F., Graubard S. (a cura di) (1974), *Il caso italiano*, Milano: Garzanti.
Geertz C. (1977), *The Interpretation of Cultures*, New York: Basic Books.
George A. L. (1969), "The 'Operational Code': A Neglected Approach to the Study of Political Leaders and Decision-Making," *International Studies Quarterly* 13(2): 190–222.
Gilbert M., Pasquino G. (a cura di) (2000), *Politica in Italia*, Bologna: il Mulino.
Glenn J., Howlett D., Poore S. (eds.) (2004), *Neorealism Versus Strategic Culture*, Aldershot, UK: Ashgate.
Goglia L., Moro R., Nuti L. (a cura di) (2006a), *Guerra e pace nell'Italia del novecento*, Bologna: il Mulino.
Goglia L., Moro R., Nuti L. (2006b), "Introduzione," in Goglia, Moro, Nuti (a cura di) (2006a).
Goldstein J., Keohane R. O. (eds.) (1993), *Ideas and Foreign Policy: Beliefs, Institutions, and Political Change*, Ithaca, NY: Cornell University Press.
Graglia P. (2006), "Europeismo: alternativa o antidoto alla guerra?" in Goglia, Moro, Nuti (a cura di) (2006a).
Gray C. (1981), "National Style in Strategy: The American Example," *International Security* 6(2): 21–47.
Gray C. (1984), "Comparative Strategic Culture," *Parameters* winter: 26–33.
Gray C. (1999), "Strategic Culture as Context: the First Generation of Theory Strikes Back," *Review of International Studies* 25(1): 49–69.
Gray C., Payne K. B. (1980), "Victory is Possible," *Foreign Policy* summer: 14–27.
Graziano L. (1968), *La politica estera italiana nel dopoguerra*, Padova: Marsilio.
Graziano L., Tarrow S. (a cura di) (1979), *La crisi italiana*, Torino: Einaudi.
Greco E. (2000), "La politica italiana durante il conflitto in Kosovo," in Aliboni, Bruni, Colombo, Greco (a cura di) (2000).
Haas P. (1992), "Introduction: Epistemic Communities and International Policy Coordination," *International Organization* 46(1): 1–35.
Hagan J. (1995), "Domestic Political Explanations in the Analysis of Foreign Policy," in Neack, Hey, Haney (ed.) (1995).
Haglund D. (2009), "What Good is Strategic Culture?" in Johnson, Kartchner, Larsen (eds.) (2009).
Halperin M. H. (1974), *Bureaucratic Politics and Foreign Policy*, Washington, DC: Brookings Institution.

Hellman S., Pasquino G. (a cura di) (1992), *Politica in Italia*, Bologna: il Mulino.
Hermann C. F., Kegley C. W., Rosenau J. (eds.) (1987), *New Directions in the Study of Foreign Policy*, London: HarperCollins.
Hermann R. G. (1996), "Identity, Norms, and National Security: The Soviet Foreign Policy Revolution and the End of the Cold War," in Katzenstein (ed.) (1996a).
Herz J. (1950), "Idealist Internationalism and the Security Dilemma," *World Politics* 2(2): 157–80.
Hobden S., Hobson J. M. (eds.) (2002), *Historical Sociology of International Relations*, Cambridge, UK: Cambridge University Press.
Hobson J. M. (2002), "What's at Stake in 'Bringing Historical Sociology Back into International Relations'? Trascending 'Chronofetishism' and 'Tempocentrism' in International Relations," in Hobden, Hobson (eds.) (2002).
Howard M. (1986), "Men against Fire: The Doctrine of the Offensive in 1914," in Paret (ed.) (1986).
Huntington S. P. (1961), *The Common Defense*, New York: Columbia University Press.
IAI (Istituto Affari Internazionali) (1993), *L'Italia nella politica internazionale, anno diciannovesimo*, Milano: Franco Angeli.
Ignazi, P., Giacomello, G., and Coticchia, F. (2012) *Italian Military Operations Abroad: Just Don't Call it War*. London: Palgrave-Macmillan.
Ilari V. (1986), "Storia politica del movimento pacifista in Italia," in Jean (a cura di) (1986).
Jacobsen C. G. (ed.) (1990), *Strategic Power: USA/USSR*, New York: St. Martin Press.
Jean C. (1995), *Geopolitica*, Bari-Roma: Laterza.
Jean C. (1990), *Studi strategici*, Milano: Franco Angeli.
Jean C. (a cura di) (1986), *Sicurezza e difesa*, Milano: Franco Angeli.
Jean C. (a cura di) (1989), *Storia delle Forze Armate italiane dalla ricostruzione postbellica alla "ristrutturazione" del 1975*, Milano: Giuffrè.
Jepperson R., Wendt A., Katzenstein P. (1996), "Norms, Identity, and Culture in National Security," in Katzenstein (ed.) (1996a).
Johnson J. L., Kartchner K. M., Larsen J. E. (eds.) (2009), *Strategic Culture and Weapons of Mass Descruction*, Basingstoke, UK: Palgrave Macmillan.
Johnston A. I. (1995a), "Thinking about Strategic Culture," *International Security* 19(4): 32-64.
Johnston A. I. (1995b), *Cultural Realism: Strategic Culture and Grand Strategy in Chinese History*, Princeton: Princeton University Press.
Johnston A. I. (1996), "Cultural Realism and Strategy in Maoist China," in Katzenstein (ed.) (1996a).
Johnston A. I. (1998a), "International Structures and Chinese Foreign Policy," in Kim (ed.) (1998).
Johnston A. I. (1998b), "China's Interstate Dispute Behaviour 1949–1992: A First Cut at the Data," *The China Quarterly* no. 193: 1–30.
Johnston A. I. (1999), "Strategic Cultures Revisited: Reply to Colin Gray," *Review of International Studies* 25(1): 519–23.
Johnston A. I. (2008), *Social States. China in International Institutions, 1980–2000*, Princeton: Princeton University Press.
Jones D. M., Bremer S. A., Singer J. D. (1996), "Militarized Interstate Disputes, 1816–1992: Rationale, Coding Rules, and Empirical Patterns," *Conflict Management and Peace Science* 15(2): 163–212.
Kahler M. (1979–1980), "Rumors of War: The 1914 Analogy," *Foreign Affairs* 58: 374–396.
Kahn H. (1965), *On Escalation*, New York: Praeger.
Katzenstein P. (1993), "Coping with Terrorism: Norms and Internal Security in Germany and Japan," in Goldstein, Keohane (eds.) (1993).
Katzenstein P. (ed.) (1996a), *The Culture of National Security*, New York: Columbia University Press.

Katzenstein P. (1996b), "Introduction: Alternative Perspectives on National Security," In Katzenstein (ed.) (1996a).
Katzenstein P., Okawara N. (1993), "Japan's National Security: Structures, Norms, and Policies," *International Security* 17(4): 84–118.
Keohane R. O., Nye J. (1989), *Power and Interdependence*, Boston: Little, Brown.
Kier E. (1995), "Culture and Military Doctrine: France Between the Wars," *International Security* 19(4): 65–93.
Kier E. (1996), "Culture and French Military Doctrine Before World War II," in Katzenstein (ed.) (1996a).
Kim S. S. (ed.) (1998), *China and the World: Chinese Foreign Policy Faces the New Millennium*, Boulder, CO: Westview Press.
Kirchner E., Sperling J. (eds.) (2007), *Global Security Governance: Competing Perceptions of Security in the 21st Century*, London: Routledge.
Kirchner E., Sperling J. (eds.) (2010), *National Security Culture*, London: Routledge.
Kissinger H. A. (1957), *Nuclear Weapons and Foreign Policy*, New York: Harper.
Klein B. S. (1988), "Hegemony and Strategic Culture: American Power Projection and Alliance Defence Politics," *Review of International Studies* 14(2): 133–48.
Klein Y. (1991), "A Theory of Strategic Culture," *Comparative Strategy* 10(1): 3–23.
Knox M. (1991), "Il fascismo e la politica estera italiana," in Bosworth, Romano (a cura di) (1991).
Kogan N. (1963), *The Politics of Italian Foreign Policy*, New York: Frederick A. Praeger.
Koslowski R., Karatochwil F. (1994), "Understanding Change in International Politics: The Soviet Empire's Demise and the International System," *International Organization* 48(4): 613–44.
Krasner S. (1978), *Defending the National Interest*, Princeton, NJ: Princeton University Press.
Lantis J. (2009), "Strategic Culture: From Clausewitz to Constructivism," in Johnson, Kartchner, Larsen (eds.) (2009).
Levy J. (1994), "Learning and Foreign Policy," *International Organization* 48(2): 279–312.
Lind J. M. (2004), "Pacifism or Passing the Buck: Testing Theories of Japanese Security Policy," *International Security* 29(1): 91–121.
Lobell S., Ripsman N., Taliaferro J. (eds.) (2009), *Neoclassical Realism, the State, and Foreign Policy*, Cambridge, UK: Cambridge University Press.
Luttwak E. (1984), *The Pentagon and the Art of War*, New York: Simon and Schuster.
MacIsaac D. (1986), "Voices from the Central Blue: The Air Power Theorists," in Paret (ed.) (1986).
MAE (Ministero degli Affari Esteri) (2009), *L'Italia e l'impegno multilaterale*, Roma.
Mahnken T. G. (2009), "U.S. Strategic and Organizational Subcultures," in Johnson, Kartchner, Larsen (eds.) (2009).
Mammarella G., Cacace P. (2008), *La politica estera dell'Italia: dallo stato unitario ai giorni nostri*, Bari-Roma: Laterza.
March J., Olsen J. P. (1989), *Rediscovering Institutions*, New York: Free Press.
May E., Neustadt R. (1986), *Thinking in Time: The Uses of History for Decision Makers*, New York: Free Press.
Mayer A. (1981), *The Persistence of the Old Regime: Europe to the Great War*, London: Croom Helm.
Mayer G. (1989), "L'evoluzione del bilancio della difesa dal 1945 al 1975," in Jean (a cura di) (1989).
Mershon C., Pasquino G. (a cura di) (2004), *Politica in Italia*, Bologna: il Mulino.
Meyer J., Boli J., Thomas G., Ramirez F. (1997), "World Society and the Nation-State," *American Journal of Sociology* 103(1): 144–81.
Miege J. L. (1976), *L'imperialismo coloniale italiano*, Milano: Rizzoli.
Minniti F. (2006), "Il sogno della grande potenza," in Goglia, Moro, Nuti (a cura di) (2006a).
Monzali L. (2005), "Riflessioni sulla cultura della diplomazia italiana in epoca liberale e fascista," in Petracchi (a cura di) (2005).

Moravcsik A. (1997), "Taking Preferences Seriously: A Liberal Theory of International Politics," *International Organization* 51(4): 513–53.
Morgenthau H. (1948), *Politics amog Nations*, New York, Knopf.
Moro R. (2006), "I cattolici italiani tra pace e guerra: dall'inizio del secolo al Concilio Vaticano II," in Goglia, Moro, Nuti (a cura di) (2006a).
Murray D. J., Viotti P. R. (eds.) (1989), *The Defense Policies of Nations*, Baltimore: Johns Hopkins University Press.
Neack L., Hey J., Haney P. (ed.) (1995), *Foreign Policy Analysis*, Englewood Cliffs, NJ: Prentice Hall.
Nones M. (1989), "L'industria militare dalla ricostruzione all'espansione," in Jean (a cura di) (1989).
Nuti L. (2006), "Linee generali della politica di difesa italiana (1945–1989)," in Goglia, Moro, Nuti (a cura di) (2006a).
Olivi B. (1978), *Carter e L'Italia. La politica estera americana, l'Europa e i comunisti italiani*, Milano: Longanesi.
Panebianco A. (1977), "La politica estera italiana: un modello interpretative," *Il Mulino* XXVI: 845–79.
Panebianco A. (1982), "Le cause interne del basso profilo," *Politica internazionale* X: 15–21.
Panebianco A. (1997), *Guerrieri democratici*, Bologna: il Mulino.
Paret P. (ed.) (1986), *Makers of Modern Strategy: from Machiavelli to the Nuclear Age*, Princeton, NJ: Princeton University Press.
Pasquino G. (1974), "Pesi internazionali e contrappesi nazionali," in Cavazza, Graubard (a cura di) (1974).
Pasquino G. (2002), *Il sistema politico italiano*, Bologna: Bononia University Press.
Perani G., Pianta M. (1992), "L'acquisto di armamenti in Italia," in De Cecco, Pianta (a cura di) (1992).
Petracchi G. (a cura di) (2005), *Uomini e nazioni. Cultura e politica estera nell'Italia del Novecento*, Udine: Gaspari.
Pianta M., Perani G. (1991), *L'industria militare in Italia*, Roma: Edizioni Associate.
Pirani P. (2004), "Political Culture and Italian Security Policy: The Bosnian Case," paper presented for the annual conference of the *Midwest Political Science Association*, April 18, 2004, Chicago.
Pirani P. (2008), "'The Way We Were': Continuity and Change in Italian Political Culture," *Political Studies Association* (http://www.psa.Ac.uk/journals/pdf5/2008/pirani.pdf).
Pons S. (2005), "La trasformazione della cultura politica del PCI nelle relazioni internazionali, 1968–1989," in Petracchi (a cura di) (2005).
Poore S. (2004), "Strategic Culture," in Glenn, Howlett, Poore (eds.) (2004).
Posner A. R. (1977), "Italy: Dependence and Policy Fragmentation," *International Organization* 31(4): 809–36.
Rallo J. (1989), "Italy," in Murray, Viotti (eds.) (1989).
Ramoino P. P. (1989), "La dottrina d'impiego delle forze navali (1945–1975)," in Jean (a cura di) (1989).
Risse-Kappen T. (ed.) (1995), *Bringing Transnational Relations Back in*, Cambridge, UK: Cambridge University Press.
Risse-Kappen T. (1996), "Collective Identity in a Democratic Community: The Case of NATO," in Katzenstein (ed.) (1996a).
Rochat G. (1971), "Il controllo politico delle forze armate dall'unità d'Italia alla seconda guerra mondiale," in De Benedetti F. et al. (a cura di) (1971).
Romano S. (2002), *Guida alla politica estera italiana*, Milano: Rizzoli.
Ronzitti (a cura di) (1977), *La politica estera italiana: autonomia, interdipendenza, integrazione e sicurezza*, Milano: Ed. Comunità.
Rosa P. (a cura di) (2003a), *Le relazioni internazionali contemporanee*, Roma: Carocci.
Rosa P. (2003b), "Introduzione: il dibattito contemporaneo nello studio delle relazioni internazionali," in Rosa (a cura di) (2003a).

Rosa P. (2006), *Sociologia politica delle scelte internazionali. Un'analisi comparata delle politiche estere nazionali*, Bari-Roma: Laterza.
Rosa P. (2010), *Lo stile del Drago. Processi e modelli della politica estera cinese*, Soveria Mannelli: Rubbettino.
Rosen S. (1995), "Military Effectiveness: Why Society Matters," *International Security* 19(4): pp. 5–31.
Rosenberg D. (1983), "The Origins of Overkill: Nuclear Weapons and American Strategy, 1945–1960," *International Security* 7(4): 3–71.
Ruggie J. (1997), "The Past as Prologue? Interest, Identity, and American Foreign Policy," *International Security* 21(4): 89–125.
Rusconi G. E. (2005a), *L'azzardo del 1915. Come l'Italia decide la sua guerra*, Bologna: il Mulino.
Rusconi G. E. (2005b), "Politica estera, interesse e identità nazionale nella Repubblica dei partiti," in Petracchi (a cura di) (2005).
Sagan S. D. (1996/1997), "Why do States Build Nuclear Weapons? Three Models in Search of a Bomb," *International Security* 21(3): 54–86.
Sampson M. (1987), "Cultural Influences on Foreign Policy," in Hermann, Kegley, Rosenau (eds.) (1987).
Santoro C. M. (1991), *La politica estera di una media potenza: l'Italia dall'Unità a oggi*, Bologna: il Mulino.
Santoro C. M. (a cura di) (1992), *L'elmo di Scipio. Studi sul modello di difesa italiano*, Bologna: il Mulino.
Schelling T. (1963), *The Strategy of Conflict*, New York: Oxford University Press.
Schilling W. R., Hammond P. Y., Snyder G. H. (eds.) (1962) *Strategy, Politics and Defense Budgets*, New York: Columbia University Press.
Schilling W. R. (1962), "The Politics on National Defense: Fiscal 1950," in Schilling, Hammond, Snyder (eds.) (1962).
Schumpeter J. (1972), *Sociologia dell'imperialismo*, Bari: Laterza.
Schweller R. (2009), "Neoclassical Realism and State Mobilization: Expansionist Ideology in the Era of Mass Politics," in Lobell, Ripsman, Taliaferro (eds.) (2009).
Serra E. (1990), *L'Italia e le grandi alleanze nel tempo dell'imperialismo*, Milano: Franco Angeli.
Silvestri S. (1990), "L'Italia: partner fedele ma di basso profilo," in Caligaris (a cura di) (1990).
Snyder J. (1977), *The Soviet Strategic Culture: Implications for Limited Nuclear Operations*, Santa Monica, CA: RAND.
Snyder J. (1984), *The Ideology of the Offensive. Military Decision-making and the Disasters of 1914*, Ithaca, NY: Cornell University Press.
Snyder J. (1990), "The Concept of Strategic Culture: Caveat Emptor," in Jacobsen (ed.) (1990).
Snyder G. H. (1962), "The 'New Look' of 1953," in Schilling, Hammond, Snyder (eds.) (1962).
Soetendorp B. (1999), *Foreign Policy in the European Union: Theory, History and Practice*, Longman: London.
Stefani F. (1989), "La dottrina d'impiego delle forze aeroterrestri," in Jean (a cura di) (1989).
Sullivan P. L., Koch M. T. (2009), "Military Intervention by Powerful States, 1945–2003," *Journal of Peace Research* 46(5): 709–18.
Swidler A. (1986), "Culture in Action: Symbols and Strategies," *American Sociological Review* 51(2): 273–86.
Van Evera S. (1984), "The Cult of the Offensive and the Origins of the First World War," *International Security* 9(1): 58–107.
Varsori A. (1998), *L'Italia nelle relazioni internazionali dal 1943 al 1992*, Bari-Roma: Laterza.
Vasquez J. (1985), "Domestic Contention on Critical Foreign-Policy Issues: The Case of the United States," *International Organization* 39(4): 643–66.

Vasquez J. (1987), "Foreign Policy, Learning, and War," in Hermann, Kegley, Rosenau (eds.) (1987).
Vasquez J. (1993), *The War Puzzle*, Cambridge, UK: Cambridge University Press.
Vigezzi B. (1991), "L'Italia dopo l'Unità: liberalismo e politica estera," in Bosworth, Romano (a cura di) (1991).
Waltz K. N. (1979) *Theory of International Politics*, Boston: McGraw-Hill.
Welch D. (2005), *Painful Choices: A Theory of Foreign Policy Change*, Princeton, NJ: Princeton University Press.
Wendt A. (1992), "Anarchy is What States Make of It," *International Organization* 46(2): 391–425.
Wendt A. (1999), *Social Theory of International Politics*, Cambridge, UK: Cambridge University Press.
Wohlstetter A. (1959), "The Delicate Balance of Terror," *Foreign Affairs* 37: 211–34.
Yost C. (1972), *The Conduct and Misconduct of Foreign Affairs*, New York: Random House.

Index

Adler, Emanuel, 29n11
Aga Rossi, Elena, 85, 86, 94n44
Aidid, Mohammed, 117
Ajello, Aldo, 116
Albonetti, Achille, 12n1
Alekseev, Mikahil, 41
Aliboni, Roberto, 115, 124, 126n19
Allison, Graham T., 12n2, 20
Andreotti, Giulio, 83, 114, 115
Annan, Kofi, 120
Arpino, Mario, 89, 94n51
Attinà, Fulvio, 110, 111, 126n8
Avarna, Giuseppe, 65

Bagnato, Bruna, 94n46
Banfield, Edward, 13n12
Barié, Ottavio, 92n24
Barnett, Michael, 28n3, 28n9
Barre, Siad, 116
Battistelli, Fabrizio, 80
Bellucci, Paolo, 119
Benedict, Ruth, 31–34, 34, 55n1, 56n17
Berger, Thomas, 46–48, 53, 56n16, 77
Berlinguer, Enrico, 2, 12n4
Berlusconi, Silvio, 122, 123
Beasley, Ryan, 1
Bin Laden, Osama, 121
Bismarck, Otto von, 64
Bollati, Riccardo, 65
Bonvicini, Gianni, 124
Booth, Ken, 41–42, 51
Bosworth, Robert J. B., 12n3
Bremer, Stuart, 96, 125n1
Bruni, Franco, 126n19
Bush, George W., 121, 123

Cacace, Paolo, 12n3, 68, 70, 75, 76, 92n23, 92n26
Cadorna, Luigi, 61, 90n3
Caligaris, Luigi, 106

Cassese, Sabino, 8, 13n16
Chabod, Federico, 5, 12n8, 63, 65, 90n6
Checkel, Jeffrey, 28n5
Colombo, Alessandro, 126n19
Conti, Guido, 67, 69, 91n11
Coralluzzo, Walter, 12n3, 13n19
Cordesman, Anthony H., 35
Crispi, Francesco, 63
Croce, Benedetto, 78
Croci, Osvaldo, 117, 120, 126n16

D'Alema, Massimo, 120
D'Amore, Ciro, 79, 93n31
Danilov, Yuri, 41
De Andreis, Marco, 126n4
De Felice, Renzo, 91n13
De Gasperi, Alcide, 74, 82–83
De Gaulle, Charles, 45
De Michelis, Gianni, 114
Desh, Michael, 31, 34, 44, 51, 56n22, 132
Deutsch, Karl, 76
Di Nolfo, Ennio, 2–3, 73, 92n21
Donovan, Mark, 115
Dossetti, Giuseppe, 82, 92n26
Dottori, Giuseppe, 10, 92n29
Dougherty, James, 81
Douhet, Giulio, 89
Dreyfus, Alfred, 39
Duffield, John, 29n12, 56n21, 56n23, 57n29
Dulles, John Foster, 94n50

Eisenhower, Dwight, 94n50
Evangelista, Matthew, 1, 28n3, 29n11

Fallières, Clément, 39
Fanfani, Amintore, 83
Fedele, Pietro, 91n12
Ferraris, Luigi V., 12n3
Finnemore, Martha, 6, 22

Focardi, Filippo, 77, 93n30
Foch, Ferdinand, 39
Foradori, Paolo, 13n9, 55n3, 90, 111, 126n5, 126n6
Forlati Picchio, Laura, 92n28
Formigoni, Guido, 82, 83, 93n40
Fortis, Alessandro, 66
Franz Ferdinand, 66
Frattini, Franco, 123
Freedman, Lawrence, 34, 94n49

Gaja, Roberto, 12n3, 87
Garruccio, Ludovico (pseudonym of Ludovico Incisa di Camerana), 5, 6, 94n52
Gasparini, Giovanni, 92n29, 121
Geertz, Clifford, 54
George, Alexander, 55n2, 93n43
Giovanni XXIII, 82
Glenn, John, 53
Goglia, Luigi, 67, 69, 89
Gorbachev, Mikahil, 27n1, 87–88
Graglia, Piero, 92n25
Gray, Colin, 38, 41, 42–44, 51, 52
Graziano, Luigi, 12n3, 92n24
Greco, Ettore, 121, 126n19, 127n21
Gronchi, Giovanni, 83, 87, 92n26
Guarino, Giuseppe,, 115

Haas, Peter, 27
Hagan, Joe, 13n13
Haglund, David, 28n10
Halperin, Morton, 12n2
Hermann, Richard, 27n1
Herz, John, 28n6
Hitler, Adolf, 67
Hobson, John, 28n9
Hötzendorf, Franz Conrad von, 66, 91n8
Howard, Michael, 55n7
Howlett, Darryl, 53
Huang, Shi Gong, 49
Huntington, Samuel, 55n9
Hussein, Saddam, 114

Ilari, Virgilio, 82, 93n37, 93n42
Imperiali, Guglielmo, 65

Jean, Carlo, 12n6, 92n27

Jepperson, Ronald, 21
Jiang, Tai Gong, 49
Joffre, Joseph, 39
Jones, Daniel, 96, 125n1
Jonhston, A. Iain, 6, 20, 25–26, 28n8, 44, 48–51, 51–54, 54, 56n20, 56n21, 56n26, 56n28, 93n36, 94n52, 125n2, 126n7, 126n9, 130–131

Kahler, Miles, 38
Kahn, Hermann, 36, 55n4
Katzenstein, Peter, 20–21, 28n3, 44, 53, 130
Kaunitz, Wenzel Anton von, 63
Kautsky, Karl, 84
Keohane, Robert O., 12n2
Kier, Elizabeth, 44–46, 53, 55n11, 56n13, 93n32, 94n52
Kissinger, Henry, 36
Klein, Bradley, 56n26
Klein, Yitzak, 56n25
Klinkhammer, Lutz, 77, 93n30
Knox, MacGregor, 68, 69, 91n14, 91n15
Koch, Michael, 126n10
Kogan, Norman, 7–8, 13n12, 94n52
Koslowski, Rey, 27n1
Krasner, Stephen, 55n8
Kratochwil, Friedrich, 27n1
Krushev, Nikita, 84

La Pira, Giorgio, 83, 93n42

Lantis, Jeffrey, 56n27
Lanza, Giovanni, 63, 65
Laporta, Piero, 10
Launay, Edoardo de, 63, 64–65
Liddel Hart, Basil, 39
Lind, Jennifer, 56n19, 93n36
Lobell, Steven, 129
Loi, Bruno, 117
Luttwak, Edward, 33
Luxemburg, Rosa, 94n45

MacIsaac, David, 89
Mahnken, Thomas G., 33
Mammarella, Giuseppe, 12n3, 68, 70, 75, 76, 92n23, 92n26
Mao, Zedong, 50–51
March, James, 23

Martino, Antonio, 122
Mattei, Enrico, 13n14, 83
May, Ernest, 24
Mayer, Arno, 40, 63
Mayer, Giorgio, 93n33, 126n4
McNamara, Robert, 43, 94n50
Mecozzi, Amedeo, 89
Metternich, Klemens von, 63
Meyer, John, 28n7
Miege, Jean, 90n5
Miggiano, Paolo, 126n4
Minghetti, Marco, 63, 65
Minniti, Fortunato, 63, 69, 70
Moltke (the Elder), Helmut von, 40
Monzali, Luciano, 65, 91n9
Moravcsik, Andrew, 12n2
Morgenthau, Hans, 91n18
Moro, Aldo, 83, 92n26
Moro, Renato, 67, 69, 81, 82, 89
Mussolini, Benito, 67–69, 73, 75, 77, 79, 91n13–91n16

Neustadt, Richard, 24
Nigra, Costantino, 63, 64
Nones, Michele, 79, 93n35
Nuti, Leopoldo, 67, 69, 89, 105, 125n3
Nye, Joseph, 12n2

O'Connor, James, 94n45
Okawara, Noburo, 28n3
Olivi, Bino, 12n4
Olsen, Johan P., 23

Pacciardi, Randolfo, 79
Panebianco, Angelo, 7, 8–9
Paolo VI, 82
Parri, Ferruccio, 74
Pasquino, Gianfranco, 2, 13n17
Payne, Keith, 38
Perani, Giulio, 80, 105
Pfaltzgraff, Robert, 81
Pianta, Mario, 80, 105
Pio XII, 82
Pirani, Piero, 6, 10, 94n54, 119
Pons, Silvio, 86
Poore, Stuart, 53, 56n21
Posner, Alan R., 13n11, 13n15
Prodi, Romano, 13n18, 123, 127n27

Rallo, Joseph, 79
Ramoino, Pier Paolo, 88, 94n51
Ripsmann, Norrin, 129
Risse, Thomas, 28n3, 93n41
Robilant, Mario di, 63, 65
Rochat, Giorgio, 79
Rognoni, Virginio, 114, 115
Romano, Sergio, 12n3, 12n7, 88, 92n23
Ronzitti, Natalino, 12n3
Rosa, Paolo, 13n9, 13n15, 13n20, 28n2, 28n4, 55n3, 90, 111, 126n5, 126n6
Rosen, Steven, 28n3
Rosenberg, David A., 94n50
Ruggie, John, 76
Rumi, Giorgio, 93n40
Rusconi, Gian Enrico, 74, 90n2, 90n3, 91n16, 97

Sagan, Scott, 23, 24
Salandra, Antonio, 65
Sampson, Martin, 21
San Giuliano, Antonio di, 65
Santoro, Carlo M., 4–5, 12n3, 12n5, 91n8, 93n34, 106, 126n4
Savoy, Carlo Alberto of, 66
Scalfaro, Oscar Luigi, 119
Scartezzini, Riccardo, 55n3
Schelling, Thomas, 35
Schilling, Werner, 92n19
Schlesinger, James, 35–36, 36
Schlieffen, Alfred von, 39, 40, 61
Schumpeter, Joseph, 63
Schweller, Randall, 65, 91n10, 97
Segni, Antonio, 83
Serra, Enrico, 90n7
Silvestri, Stefano, 10, 92n27
Sima, Rangiu, 49
Singer, David, 96, 125n1
Siniora, Fouad, 124
Snyder, Glenn H., 35, 94n50
Snyder, Jack, 36–38, 39–41, 51, 56n24, 131
Soetendorp, Ben, 10
Sonnino, Sidney, 65
Spadolini, Giovanni, 106
Stefani, Filippo, 88, 94n48
Sturzo, Luigi, 82
Sullivan, Patricia, 126n10
Sun, Zi, 49

Swidler, Ann, 46, 55n12, 93n36, 94n52

Taliaferro, Jeffrey, 129
Talleyrand, Charles Maurice de, 64
Taviani, Paolo Emilio, 83
Tittoni, Tommaso, 65
Truman, Harry, 74

Varsori, Antonio, 12n3, 92n23, 92n24
Vasquez, John, 24–25, 47, 71–73, 91n17, 110, 131
Ven Evera, Stephen, 38–39, 131
Vigezzi, Brunello, 65

Visconti Venosta, Emilio, 63, 65
Vittorio, Emanuele II, 63, 65

Waltz, Kenneth N., 18, 20
Wei, Liao, 49
Wendt, Alexander, 17–19, 21, 22, 28n5
Wohlstetter, Albert, 34
Wu, Qi, 49

Yost, Charles, 13n13

Zaslavsky, Victor, 85, 86, 94n44

About the Author

Paolo Rosa is associate professor of political science in the Department of Sociology and Social Research, and the School of International Studies of the University of Trento, Italy. He is an associate of the EU Non-Proliferation Consortium. His main research interests include foreign policy analysis, Italian foreign policy, Chinese politics, and strategic culture.